LEGACY – A New Season

by John T. Wills

The story within the pages of this novel is a fictional account with all characters created for the purposes of this literary work. Any similarities to persons living or dead, places or events other than those occurrences in the public domain are purely accidental and unintended.

ISBN: 0615655505
ISBN-13: 9780615655505

Very Special Thanks

It is with great pleasure that I give special recognition to the following people for their tremendous support. I could not have done this without you.

Elijah Gomer-Wills

Jamie & Danielle Barrett

Faye Harrison

Ms. T

With all of my heart, I thank you from the bottom of my heart!!!

Dedication

To My Legacy

I am extremely proud of my beloved grandson and honored to dedicate this novel to my "Legacy" - Elijah Gomer-Wills. My son, Rashad Ali Wills, departed this life on my grandson's first birthday; a horrible start to his young life. I've cried many tears since that fateful day. I am a living witness that no parent should ever have to bury a child. Trust and believe losing a child is the most dreadful experience any parent can endure - if you can endure it because the pain does not go away. But I have come to know that an authority greater than all of us controls such adversity.

I am grateful that God blessed me with my son and his benevolent gift of a very special grandson. Words cannot express my love or commitment to this child, who I credit with saving my life after Rashad's death. Without hesitation, I will give my life for him. With that said, I pledge to give the rest of my life to him. I feel duty bound to impart my wisdom unto his spirit, enabling him to grow into manhood, as my grandfather did with me.

My grandfather taught me two very important life lessons. The first lesson was "I raised you to be a man; you don't know what you might do as a man, but when the time comes – you do it." The second was "the difference between a man and a boy is the lessons he learns." I promise that my grandson will, without a doubt, learn these lessons too. Moreover, I want to teach him this: "some things are impossible; some things are obstacles; but a wise man will try to overcome both because, as it is written, God bless the child that's got his own."

From my heart, I plead the blood of our Lord and I transcend my soul unto him for he is the light and the love of my life. Therefore I have promised Elijah, like the mythological Phoenix, my "Legacy" will rise from the ashes of sorrow and soar; for he is the winter, fall, and spring of a New Season.

John T. Wills
Granddad

Miss Me – But Let Me Go

When I have come to the end of the road
and the sun has set for me.
I want no rites in a gloom filled room.
Why cry for a soul set free.
Miss me a little, but not for long
and not with your head bowed low.
Remember all the good times we shared.
Miss me but let me go.
For this journey we all must take
and each must go alone. I'll be alright Dad.
It's all part of God's plan and
just a step on the road home.
When you are missing me and your heart is pained.
Go to the friends we know
and bury your sorrows in doing so.
I will be waiting for you.
Miss me but let me go.

(Author Unknown)

Jesus said, *"I am the resurrection and the life. He who believes in me will live, even though he dies; Whoever... believes in me will never die."*
John 11:25-26

R.I.P.

Rashad Ali Wills

Contents

Forward

The book you are holding is a sequel, so let me start by offering praise for its predecessor, *Just a Season*, the debut novel written by John T. Wills. John is a relatively new author and a very good writer. He is also someone for whom I have much respect. As soon as I read the raw, unedited pages of *Just a Season*, I was hooked. I knew it was a historical narrative and sensed it was based on real lives and real events.

I cannot say enough about this profoundly thought provoking literary work that is a genuine page-turner. What surprised me as I got involved in the completion of its publication was how it would change me. It allowed me a glimpse, a little insight into the soul of the author and the soul of a people, and for that I am very grateful. The time I spent with *Just a Season* remains one of the more profound periods of my life.

It has been several years since *Just a Season*, and it's time to move on. "*Legacy – A New Season*" is both continuation and a stand-alone story. Generations have come and gone, life is bearable after all, and hope lives in a little boy and in a man who almost lost all hope.

Eunice Course
"The Saint"

Just a Season is the predecessor to ***Legacy – A New Season.*** It is a luminous story into the life of a man who, in the midst of pain and loss, journeys back in time to reexamine all the important people, circumstances, and intellectual fervor that contributed to the richness of his life. It is a must read novel that will cause you to see the world through new eyes.

This fictional narrative begins with a grief-stricken father visiting the gravesite of his beloved son who was killed in a tragic accident; a moment that he and no other loving parent should ever have to face. As he sadly gazes at his son's headstone and reads what is inscribed there, the dates 1981 - 2001 bring about an illuminating discovery.

The tiny dash that separates the years of one's birth and death represents the whole of a person's life. If this tiny dash were to tell his life's story, what would it say? In "*Just a Season*", the dash of this man's life is revealed and what emerges from the pages of this book is a legacy of true benevolence and grace. This is not a story you will read, it is a story that you will live as you travel in time through this man's eyes as he vividly relives his legacy. It's the journey of a lifetime that lives on...

Praise for "JUST A SEASON"

"Thank you for your example of tenderness and discipline in what I know is a story of love, delicately shared with readers in a way that says, this life, though brief, is significant. So hold it in highest regard for "the dash" is our legacy to love ones, indeed to the world, which we are blessed to share, albeit, for *Just a Season*." Excellent!

Sistah Joy, Poet, Cable TV Host

"... You feel as if you somehow become an invisible character in the unfolding of this epic narration."

Silver Rae Fox, Actress, Model, Radio Personality

"... this is the stuff movies are made of... not since "Roots" have I read anything that so succinctly chronicles an African American story." Amazing!

Cheryl, Avid Reader

"Wills pulls you in from the very first page... *Just a Season* is a heart-wrenching story about growing up and believing in yourself."

Cheryl Hayes, APOOO Book Club

"Not since The Color Purple have I read a book that evoked such emotions. John T. Wills possesses the ability to transport the reader directly into the life and struggles of his main characters story.

Tonja Covington

"JUST A SEASON is laced with thought-provoking commentary on the Vietnam War, the assassinations of the 1960s, the migration of crack cocaine into inner-city neighborhoods, and a myriad of other ills that have rocked America. This is a very good piece intertwined with several history lessons spanning many decades."

Dawn Reeves, RAWSISTAZ Book Club

"John T. Wills particulars each notion so eloquently that you feel that you're actually right there with him... this is an inflicting history lesson that I believe all African American males should experience." *JUST A SEASON* is a pivotal read.

Carmen, OOSA ONLINE BOOK CLUB

"From the first page you are transported into John's world as if you are there and are experiencing it with him. I thoroughly enjoyed *"Just a Season"*.

Mia L. Haynes

"Just a Season is a work of love, respect and honor... A book filled with the wonder of life, and the pain and growth encountered in living it." Outstanding!

Ron Watson, Editor, New Book Reviews.Org

Be sure to get this
Must Read Novel
and now the story continues...

http://johntwills.com

Prelude

If you were to reexamine the time in which you've lived, you will come to know that the reason we live is to die. The question then becomes what happens between the years of one's birth and death. This is without question a quandary that each of us will face. In the novel "*Just a Season*", I referred to this specific period of earthly existence as the dash that will be placed on our final marker between the beginning and end dates of life's journey. This period of time can only be characterized as a journey because this tiny little dash represents the whole of a person's life.

It's been said, there are no words that have not been spoken and there are no stories that have never been told, but there are some you will not forget. *Just a Season* is that story. It chronicles what has been called a contemporary "Roots" with a reviewer saying "this is the stuff movies are made of... I have not read anything that so succinctly chronicles an African American story." Another reviewer said, "Not since The Color Purple have I read a book that evoked such emotions… transports the reader directly into the life and struggles of the main characters..."

I am honored to have been chosen to channel such an epic saga to the world. With that said, I am reminded of a powerful statement once made during a sermon by my childhood pastor - Reverend Cole. He said, "Unless and until you suffer enough pain, then and only then, will you reach deep inside and feel the breath that God has breathed into your soul coming eye to eye with your destiny". I've pondered that profound statement my entire life and it continues to deeply impact my life.

It could very well be because I've lost my son that I have come to embrace this message so profoundly. There have been a number of reflections from those early days at Friendly Church that continue to touch my spirit. Specifically: "Why Jesus wept?" As the story goes, Jesus was so moved as he witnessed the pain of Mary and Martha weeping for the loss of his dear friend, Lazarus, that he also wept. Today, I understand that emotion because I have felt such pain. This might explain why I was chosen as the vehicle to share such a powerful story that will surely live far beyond the season I've been given.

Just a Season is a historical narrative that begins with a grief-stricken father visiting the gravesite of his beloved son who was killed in a tragic automobile accident - a dreadful moment no loving parent should ever have to face. The main character, John Wells, asks himself a philosophical question as he views his late son's final marker. "If the tiny dash placed on my marker were to tell my life's story, what would it say?"

What emerged from the pages is a legacy of true benevolence and grace that I believe is destined to be become a literary classic. This luminous story is a riveting portrait into the life of an African American man who, in the midst of pain and loss, journeys back in time to reexamine all the important people, events, circumstances, and intellectual fervor that contributed to the richness of his life. Moreover, the main character relives all of the significant events affecting the African-American Diaspora, over a fifty-year period, providing a perspective of reality to the unfolding history.

As the story ends, as if in the blink of an eye, John reflects upon his life's journey realizing the irony that we come into the world crying while all around us are smiling. Then, we leave the world smiling while everybody around us weeps. This thought causes him to recall another powerful sermon Reverend Cole gave explaining this phenomenon in the simplest of terms. The Good Reverend said, "This period of existence that we call life in the final analysis is *Just a Season."* Then with a deep sigh realizing that the story must end, as stories do, he leaves the cemetery slowly walking past his loved ones resting for eternity; pausing briefly to look back in the direction of his son's resting place and says, "I will always love you."

As he nears the crest of the hill walking into the abyss of time, he pauses at his grandfather's resting place, seemingly unable to take the next step. With tears flowing down his face, he gently touches the headstone of his grandfather and quietly asks him "to look after my son". At that moment, he fondly recalls the last thing his grandfather said; "life is not just a race you run. It is a relay. It is now your responsibility to pass the baton." Somehow, John finds the strength to look toward the heavens and say softly that "I have to be Granddaddy now. I just hope my grandson will love me as much as I loved you. More importantly, I must make sure that he tells his grandchildren about me."

It's been several years since this epiphany led me to tell the story of this man's epic journey that many have wondered if it was a true story, miracle, a blessing or simply a fairy tale. I will only say that "*Just a Season*" is a must-read story that reflects the audacity of hope, pain, and struggle of a people. It will most assuredly touch every emotion as you travel through time, as you relive a life through the eyes of an African American man living in America.

At the story's end, John sorrowfully leaves the cemetery at Friendly Church that day feeling as if God has forsaken him. But his conviction is strong in faith and he knows that faith is the instrument to believe true what is not seen. With all the strength within, he refuses to drown in his tears; rather he is committed to swim in his blessings knowing that God has not forsaken him because the wonders of life spoke loudly. Blessed are those who believe and have not seen which is tomorrow and tomorrow holds his "*Legacy and A New Season*"...

Chapter One

We travel through the reality of time known as life. This reality begins at birth much in the way the journey of a thousand miles begins with a single step. With that said, I will admit, like that first step, over the course of my existence that journey has been trying at times, sometimes rewarding, and always challenging. Maybe this is why I always seem to return to this place that has spiritually grounded me throughout this journey. That place is within the confines of Friendly Church. I've always found it interesting that no matter how far or where I've traveled, it always beckons and, for some reason, it feels like home comforting my soul. I suppose it's the mystical cord of my memory connecting me to my soul.

It's a crisp, almost cold, fall morning that has the feel of impending snow. The autumn air is somewhat hazy and the sky, slightly overcast. I find myself sitting somberly, all alone, in the first pew - hours before any of the good Christian folk show up for the Sunday morning service. My eyes are focused upward at an empty pulpit surrounded by a choir loft that seems to emit the angelic sounds of my favorite hymn - "I feel like going on". I look at the empty podium before me, awaiting the good Reverend's delivery of another powerful message that, I hope, will inject me with the strength I need to go on.

It's been sometime since God called my only son home to be with him and the pain of his absence does not go away. No parent should have to bury a child, let alone the only child they've been blessed to have. It just doesn't seem right for a child to go before a parent but then this is not something that is unique to me. I know from scripture that, from the beginning of time, others have endured such pain. Able died before Adam and Eve and John the Baptist died preceding his parents. We also know for certain that Jesus died before his mother Mary because she witnessed his crucifixion. How painful that must have been.

My conviction tells me that God does not make mistakes. I guess there is some comfort in this principle of thought because I am very grateful that my son blessed me with his son, Elijah, my grandson, who we call Boo. It's eerie that my son and his mother chose to give him the name of such a great biblical prophet. Maybe because he is all I have. Therefore, I am obligated to instill all of my wisdom into his soul and therefore I must help him to write his story - a story not yet written. Since I was blessed with a wonderful grandfather to teach me, it will be easy for me to share that wisdom with my grandson. Actually, it is my responsibility to provide that foundation for him as it was done for me.

So I find myself sitting here today humming that old Negro spiritual "Nobody knows the trouble I see". I believe with certainty that there is someone greater than myself, who I chose to call God. I understand that faith is being sure of what you hope for and certain of what you cannot see. I have to be honest and say that my faith has been challenged. Perhaps that's why I am entirely consumed with this emotion of uncertainty. I gaze upward, looking over the choir section at the half stained circular glass window with a picture of Jesus hanging on the cross below it.

It hurts so much because the heartache that comes with living makes the journey seem almost impossible at times, and today is one of those times. All I can do today is sit here and serenely pray for the strength to rise again. It's sort of like waiting for the rapture, to be resurrected while still existing in this earthly realm. I feel like quitting but I can't - I've got so much to do. Maybe that's why I'm here this morning because my journey has been guided by those powerful words once spoken by my grandfather, "fear not for I am with you".

Long before I was born my Granddaddy, Sylvanus Reid, had a dream. Actually, it was more of a prophecy. I was just a young child when he first uttered what he believed was an inspired declaration of his celestial will or more simply put - my purpose and his vision of my destiny. Without getting too biblical, in my eyes Granddaddy was a prophet. He made it very clear that in order to reach my full potential it was important that I be a leader – like Moses. He had the forethought of reason that led to the consciousness of what I viewed as spiritual truth. I believe this has added profoundly to the equity within my dash.

My grandfather was without a doubt the final authoritative revealer of my reason for being. I've always thought this to be some sort of divinely inspired revelation concerning my fate. I've often wondered if Granddaddy sat here in this sanctuary at Friendly Church when he conceived this notion. I can recall vividly the last thing he told me before his transition into eternity "life is not a race you run, it is a relay and you have a responsibility to pass the baton". Today I understand the meaning contained within those powerful words because I am Granddaddy now.

My Granddaddy told me every day of my life that "I raised you to be a man and as a man you don't know what you will have to do but when the time comes – do it". I have lived by this as if it was one of the Ten Commandments and my grandson hears it too. It is very important for him to understand that the difference between a man and a boy is the lessons he learns. Which, by the way, reminds me of a song that speaks to the way of the world; "a child is born with a heart of gold and the way of the world makes him oh so cold".

Somehow I must prepare my grandson for the reality that life's lessons require us to endure pain and pain simply put is the seed necessary for growth. Therefore, I must be the Gardner who nurtures the seeds.

Chapter Two

While I find solace in this moment I hear the sound of a soft deep voice echoing throughout the sanctuary that says, "You are at one with the spirit of a living God. Do not forget that the will of God will never take you where the Grace of God will not protect you." Upon hearing those comforting words I lower my head and respond through prayer - asking for the power to release and let go of all pain, past hurts, misunderstandings, and grudges. This is something that is very difficult for most humans I know and it is something that cannot be done alone.

I find myself asking for the strength to overcome the suffering and betrayals from relationships forged during my journey, particularly the pain inflected by those closest to me. One would think when you have lost a child you and your mate would grow closer. Well, that is a fallacy. I can attest to that as fact because the woman, Flo, to whom I gave so much of my life and who was mother to this child will never recover from his passing.

I discovered, or more aptly put, she revealed an alternative lifestyle to which she was released to enjoy the comfort of her woman friend. For over thirty years, I trusted and loved this woman, and I use that loosely, only to find out that she was morally challenged and narcissistic. Her wretchedness was so deeply furtive and engrained that she was able to turn the woman who birthed me and her children against me. It is heartbreaking to admit that such a malicious act of deception and treachery could reside within people I thought loved me.

I've always believed that a mother's job is to love her children unconditionally. I guess that's not a principle to which every woman subscribes. I can't help but feel violated because I am responsible for all of these people having homes, and I mean physical buildings. I gave benevolently honoring my promise as a husband. I did more than any son or brother was obligated to do. Yet, they betrayed me in the worst way, which is simply a disgrace. Surely God will be the judge of their deceitful actions.

I can only say, it is a sin and a shame that these people who profess to love God would have hearts so impure. I've asked myself many times how someone can claim to love God who they cannot see, yet cannot love a man who they can see. These people are the ones I've helped and sacrificed so much for and they ended up being the worst offenders. I feel betrayed and their actions are unforgivable.

Of course, I realize that I have to overcome this disappointment and find the strength to survive because I have so much work left to do. Therefore, I have no choice but to continue this journey without them while I await my eternal rest. What I can say is that none of this matters today because I have Elijah and all is right with the world. It's just me and Boo now.

So I must prepare my grandson for the "snake" as Granddaddy put it. Granddaddy would tell me this story about his friend who saved the life of a snake and after he had done so - the snake bit him. The old guy was shocked and asked, "Why would you do such a thing after all I've done for you?" The snake answered him bluntly saying, "I am a snake and that's what we do". What Granddaddy was teaching me, like the snake, people will hurt you because that is what they do. So Boo needs to know; "keep your enemies close and watch your friends more closely".

Trust and believe, I know pain and not just from losing my son, rather from the negative thoughts and lack of support from those closest to me during my darkest hours, which hurt more than words can say. I have learned the lessons Granddaddy taught me and understand that these things are mere vehicles sent by the enemy to kill my spirit, steal my joy, and destroy my faith. This may be the reason I have returned to my place of solace on this autumn morning to feel the healing power of Friendly Church.

As I sit here, in this peaceful sanctuary, I am again reminded of scripture. Colossians 3: 12-15 comes to mind, "as God's chosen people, hold and dearly loved, clothe yourselves with compassion, kindness, humility, gentleness and patience. Bear with each other and forgive whatever grievances you may have against one another. Forgive as the Lord forgave you. And over all these virtues put on love, which binds them all together in perfect unity. Let the peace of Christ rule in your hearts, since as members of one body you were called to peace. And be thankful."

I felt a chill come over me causing a strange sensation that seemed to enlighten my consciousness. It is the concept that love, above all things, is the healing factor necessary for my continued existence. Suddenly, what seemed like a ray of light engulfed me with its powerful aura allowing me to understand that I have been abundantly blessed!

Yes, I am blessed because today I have a reason to live; my grandson. It seemed as if I had been absorbed by grace. This spirit consumed my entire being. It crystallized my purpose and caused me to understand that with every deed you are sowing a seed. Though the harvest you may not see, it will grow mightier than thee. Then I heard the voice say "forgive them for they know not what they do".

Chapter Three

Just as sure as fried chicken was to be had after every Sunday service, the good Christian folk began to arrive with a momentous spirit of jubilation that filled the air. The power of that spirit embraced me and the good reverend did not disappoint. The service was moving and inspirational with a powerful message that provided me with a much needed sense of hope. Rarely do I mingle or fellowship after service, and today would be no different. Let me be clear, it is not because of the congregation, who I know and love dearly. Rather it's because I am private to a fault and of course my need for serenity is the more likely reason.

I separate myself from the enlightened congregation and walk down the slope of the cemetery to say hello to my son, and as always, place a flower on his grave. I kneel to say a prayer, something else I always do, and tell him that I am going to pick up Elijah. He knows how close we are. I wanted him to know that he will be spending the week with me and I know that will bring a smile. I glance over my shoulder and notice some of the church folk watching. For a brief moment I wondered if they thought this was wrong - talking to my son like this.

It really doesn't matter all that much to me what others think because it heals my soul. I want my son to know that I am there for his child because he cannot be. I look upward to the heavens and I quietly say goodbye. This always brings a tear as I turn to leave with a heavy heart. I begin to move up the slight incline and slowly stroll past Granddaddy's resting place where I always stop to ask him to look after my son.

So much has happened since my son left me. The country was in disarray. "W" or "King George" and those villains had really made a mess of things. Thankfully, someone will soon replace him as we near the end of a contentious presidential election campaign that seems to have lasted forever. Actually, it's been nearly two years, a long time, with one of the candidates being a black man. This is very significant because this guy really has a chance of winning - making him the first American president of color.

He's beaten a formidable opponent in the primaries; the wife of the man I thought was the closest we'd ever get to a black president in my lifetime – Brother Bill as I like to call him. Although I have to say Brother Bill's blackness was questioned during the campaign as he understandably supported his wife - letting us know that he was a white man after all. Yes, he digressed a few times, but all was eventually forgiven.

Now, it was a different story concerning the black man's Republican opponent. He took a page straight out of the fifties with racism being the foundation of his campaign. One of his constant themes was to continue to ask "Who is Barack Obama?" Implying or reminding his constituents that his opponent was a Negro, which I viewed as subtle compared to the war hero's running mate who came off as the real redneck. She came into the race as the pure example of white womanhood, which lasted about a week.

Then it became clear that she was about as qualified as a doorknob and just as informed. She took every opportunity to remind those of the same hue that she represented the "Real America" placating to what would become the Tea Party crowd. Caribou Barbie's placating was so transparent that Ray Charles, who is blind and dead, could see through her vain assertion of entitlement. If the campaign would have lasted a few more weeks I'm sure the "N-word" would have been spoken outwardly in reference to the Democratic candidate.

My grandson lives about an hour and a half from where I live. So during the drive to pick up Boo I had enough time to ponder the possibility that a black man might become president. My mind reflected on the reality that just maybe they would do as they have always done; somehow steal the election. I have to tell you I was proudly one of the first to be fully supportive of this black man who could become our next President. That notwithstanding, I did have mixed emotions along with some serious reservations. But I remained positive, as my hope was there would not be a repeat of the two-thousand presidential election; the result of which, practically destroyed America.

These were truly difficult times. America was involved in two wars and was about to go broke. It felt as if the world that I knew had been turned upside down. But, I held strong in my faith that the system would not deny the right man for the job; if for no other reason than there comes a time when time itself needs a change and that time was now. The long ride, plus the powerful sermon, gave me much time to envision what would be nothing short of a miracle.

I turned onto my grandson's street and pulled into his driveway. Suddenly, all of those thoughts subsided. I could see him looking through the window waiting for me. WOW, how wonderful!! It always warmed my heart to see him run to me in full gallop. I picked him up holding him tightly. He said, "Come on Granddad let's go, we've got to get ice cream". He said goodbye to his mother with his bag in hand and we walk hand in hand to the car to do what has become a ritual for us - ICE CREAM!!! When we got home, and yes my home is his home, we did what we always do, watch cartoons with popcorn for the rest of the evening.

The next day was pre-election day and the anxiety was all-encompassing. I knew my guy could win. Actually, I was praying as I watched the news throughout the day getting the latest up to the minute, blow-by-blow accounts as the candidates sprinted to the end. While the war hero and his token candidate continued their racist rants trying to sway the few last minute hypocrites, I knew it was over for them.

Just as I did with my son, Boo and I tracked the election predictions via the computer, although he did not share the same excitement about the campaign as did I. Nonetheless, this was so much cooler than it was with my son because there was an electoral map that you could use to calculate the states each candidate could win based on state polling data and the pundits' predictions. I tried every imaginable scenario and I could not see any way my guy could lose.

The thought of a black man becoming President of these United States was a bit scary knowing the horrible and dangerous history of America's past concerning race relations. It conjured up those imagines that were all too common in the sixties – assassination. I could not help but recall those turbulent years. It was very clear that there were forces with agendas and people with evil intent lurking in the shadows of the "Real America".

The next morning, the sun rose as it always did but today was very different and dare I say - special. I made sure I was the first in line at my polling place with Boo in tow. I took my Grandfather and Grandmother's pictures into the voting booth with me as I voted. I said a prayer and I swear I could hear Big Momma, my grandmother, say "today is what we've waited for and you will witness it for us". I got a chill upon hearing this revelation.

I hurriedly cast my vote, of course for Mr. Obama, and left the booth, rushing home to monitor the results. It seemed like the longest day of my life waiting for eight PM and the polls to closed. In no time at all, around 10 o'clock, the news media announced that Barack Obama has been projected to be the next President of the United States. Jubilations filled the air with instant celebrations consuming the nation.

It was presumed by most of the talking heads that the election would be close - ha - not even. My man won and I was drained from all the anticipation. I suppose I wanted to transfer my energy to my grandson as he saw me cry for the first time in his life. In spite of serving in the military and other service to America; the miracle I'd just witnessed manifested in me the realization of finally feeling like an American. It was a very surreal and frankly an indescribable feeling. I had witnessed something that no one living or dead ever thought would happen.

Chapter Four

With the dawn of a new day, America already felt like a very different place; a place where the dream of hope has been realized. On November 5th 2008, the world seemed too changed in an instant. America elected a new President – a President that looked like me. This was astonishing, a black man - a man who was the embodiment of what so many African Americans had prayed so desperately for since being dragged onto the shores of Virginia to build this country through forced labor. Ironically, the new president won the state that was once home of the Confederate capital that fought so hard to uphold the institution of slavery.

My grandson, my heart and soul, would be with me for the week and had crawled into my bed. While he snuggled up to me, I held him tightly knowing that this historic event offered so much promise for his future and that of all African Americans. This was unlike any time in the nation's long and storied history. As I admired him in his peaceful bliss of sleep I could not think of a more significant occurrence since the world began, or at least since the resurrection of Christ. Ironically, the thought of scripture came to mind, which tells us that "the first will be last and the last will be first".

As I lay there trying to wrap my mind around this miracle, I found myself wondering - did this really happen? This was an event that nobody and I repeat, nobody ever expected to see in these United States. As I ecstatically embraced the moment with much pride and great jubilation, I was profoundly uplifted for various reasons. Being a student of history, I imagined how it must have felt when the slaves in Texas got the news, two years after the Civil War ended, that they were free. A day we now call Juneteenth.

The only thing that made this day more special was that I experienced it with Boo. The bond my grandson and I share is tighter than any grandparent. That includes the bond that I shared with my Granddaddy; possibly because at the moment of my son's death Boo was with me and I was holding him in my arms. I suppose, having been blessed with what I have come to know as the most precious gift in the world, which makes me truly a blessed man. I am grateful that today Boo will have a chance to live in a world far different than that I knew living in America. It is my hope that my grandson will be spared the bigotry and racism I've known.

You see, on the night of my son's accident, the night before Boo's first birthday, he was spending the night as a birthday party was planned later that day. Yes, my son died on the morning of Boo's first birthday. So it goes without saying that he is the light of my life and the reason that I live. It was at this moment of reflection that I felt him move - rolling toward me, waking up in a manner similar to that of a baby cub on an autumn day. He yawned, looked at me with a big smile and said, "Good morning Granddad".

I wondered if he really knew the profoundness of this historic day. So I said, "No Boo it's a great morning". I found myself holding him as if I was holding on to him for dear life. Actually, I was holding on to him for his life because of the prospect of a much better life for him. One that he will now live with virtually no limits imposed upon him because the last 'White Only" sign will have been removed from the American lexicon; at least that is my hope.

Boo is a very curious little boy who is now almost eight. He reminds me of how I was during that period of my young life where I enjoyed the company of my Granddaddy. I can remember how I would ask Granddaddy question after question, just as he does with me. It's eerie the similarities comparing the two relationships. After a few more yawns, he asks me, "Why are you so happy - Granddad?" With a huge smile I ask him, "Do you know who Obama is?" "Yes Granddad, he is the new President of America." Still smiling I ask, "Do you know what that means?" "Yes Granddad", but this time he says, "He is the President of the United States".

As we laid there I thought this was a good time to explain the significance of this very special day. So I began to tell him what made this day so amazing. "Boo, people who looked like us were brought to America for one reason – to be slaves." Our ancestors were treated worse than any wretched beast that someone owned. We were robbed of our culture, history, and worst yet, some will argue, our souls. People of African descent have experienced a horrible journey and one that America does not often mention. They speak of freedom but it was not freedom for all – only those of a certain hue.

Let me start from the beginning and tell you about a day that will live in infamy. It was in the year 1619, on a warm summer's day when a strange ship rode the tide onto the shores of Virginia at a place called Jamestown. By all accounts, it was a mysterious sight because no one knew if this ship was a trader, privateer, or a man of war ship. It flew a Dutch flag as it approached the shores of the English settlement. What was different about this ship was that it carried a strange cargo; twenty chained Africans to be sold as slaves. Ironically, this was the year of the first representative assembly in the Virginia colony establishing legal enforcement of ownership.

From the moment the Africans set foot on the shore of this strange land it initiated the greatest crime the world has ever known. A government sponsored and sanctioned institution of terror that would last in one form or another to this very day. This was the beginning of a designation of an inferior position for an entire race of people for one purpose – drudgery. This strange place the slaves called "merica" was to become a brutal place for these African's to include those not yet born.

The colony was in its infancy and would become one of American's most segregated states. The white settlers were starving, needing labor, and challenged by the Indians. This period was known as "the starving times" where the few hundred white settlers were so desperate that they were forced to eat each other to survive, which was a very good indication of their amoral and brutal nature despite their morally high religious claims.

These Africans were sold as slaves that morning with the intent to be enslaved for all times. A slave, if you don't know son, is a human being held in servitude as the chattel of another for life. Africans had been brought to the Caribbean and South America prior to this landing in Virginia by the

Portuguese who introduced the concept of slavery to the new world around the mid fourteen hundreds. But it was on this morning that the dark cloud of shame cast its shadow over America.

So it was on that sad day in August that the birth of slavery in America was born, or maybe I should say, Jamestown became known, at least to me, as the scene of the crime. Just imagine being forcibly transported to a strange place having been chained and beaten during the long journey across the vast Atlantic Ocean to be sold as a beast of burden or an object of labor for the purpose of economics for life. This journey would come to be known as the "Middle Passage".

It is important to understand that, in spite of their reasons for enslaving a whole race of people; they justified their actions, in part, through biblical interpretations. Therefore, when slavery was sanctioned by the institution of the church, it was very easy to have no remorse for the inhuman treatment of another human being. Let me be clear, all of the blame for this travesty does not rest solely on the shoulders of the white slave traders and settlers. I cannot and we should not forgive the African tribal leaders and chieftains who bore a great deal of responsibility for the initiation of this crime.

They were the ones who captured and sold their brothers and fellow countryman into this wretched condition. The circumstances that led the Africans to these shores that day were more inhuman than any crime - EVER. It would begin with the capture that usually began in the interior of the continent. The captured people included men, women, and children who were force-marched to the coast, sometimes as much as 1000 miles, with shackles around their necks under whip and guns. It was a death march in which two out of five died before reaching their destination.

Those who reached the coast were shoved into pens and cages until they were sold, sometimes for weeks, often with other Africans speaking different languages. Then they were packed aboard slave ships in spaces not much bigger than coffins, chained together in the dark wet slime of the ships belly, choking on the stench of their own excrement. They were subjected to an institution of bondage that would be permanent and physically crippling, while removed from any sense of family ties and with no hope of a future.

However, the real travesty was being injected forcibly into this system that was the foundation of white supremacy; "In the name of God". I will tell you that it was greed for limitless profit that came from capitalism. This system was designed to reduce another human being to less than human stature through racial hatred, brutality and rape, grounded in the concept that whites were Masters and Blacks were slaves. This conviction was held so strongly that it was institutionalized by the Founding Fathers within the sacred Constitution of the new nation, which somehow seems to be overlooked when people speak of freedom and democracy.

Granddad, "why did the African people do this to their own people?" Well Boo, I've asked myself that question a million times; "Why would a people who were sophisticated enough to have thriving markets and enterprises, establish the first known college, expand trade routes, and hold dear what was considered civilization – do such a thing?" Africa was a continent that gave the world the thriving metropolis of Timbuktu, Mali, and great civilizations all along the Nile River. Yet, they had the moral ineptitude to be co-conspirators in such a crime. So to answer your question Boo, "I don't know."

Could they have understood how they affected millions and millions of lives as a result of their actions? When you consider the heinousness of this crime upon another human being and race of people; it was despicable. The voyage across the ocean to America was so horrible that slaves often jumped overboard to drown rather than continue their suffering. Let me say that this was the same fate a captive would receive during the voyage if they did not conform – thrown overboard. On average, one out of three slaves lived to reach the shores.

It is estimated that by 1860, fifteen million had been transported to the shores of America. It is roughly estimated that 50 million, possibly more, were captured to become slaves to include those who died before reaching America. This was nearly one third of Africa's population at the time. In the early years of slavery before racism was a designed control mechanism, their labor was used for the purpose of economics – plain and simple. Now, as you can imagine it wasn't very long before the settlers got into the slave trade because the profits became so enormous and the temptation was much too great.

It was at this time that the psychology of racism was established to create the ideology of racism as a government institution, making slavery the law of the land with all whites being superior. According to folklore, it was also around this time that the settlers sent for a man from the Caribbean to come to Virginia to plant the seeds that would last three hundred years maybe a thousand, he proclaimed. But I will talk more about this man later.

The most diabolical aspect of the system was that it was both psychological and physical at the same time. Slaves were taught discipline, made to understand in no uncertain terms the idea of their own inferiority to "know their place", to see blackness as a sign of subordination, to be awed by the power of the master, to merge their interest with the master's, and destroy their own individuality.

The slave masters used the discipline of hard labor, the breakup of the slave family, and the lulling effects of religion to effectively erase there African identity. They created disunity among slaves by separating them into field slaves and more privileged house slaves. Finally, they used the power of law and the immediate power of the overseer to invoke unthinkable brutality; whipping, burning, mutilation, and yes – death to maintain ultimate control.

What you will not be taught in school is that as this country was being formed there were laws passed to ensure that the system remained permanent and intact. For example, dismemberment was included in the Virginia Code of 1705 and Maryland passed a law in 1723 providing for cutting off the ears of blacks who struck a white person. For more serious crimes slaves would be hung and the body was quartered and exposed. I used these examples because this occurred here in our area but it was not out of the ordinary anywhere in the country.

So you see Boo, most jurisdictions had measures or laws established to protect the property and the investment in human souls, created by a complex web of historical threads to support this wretched system. Granddad, "Why would people do these things?" Well son, greed and the lack of morality gives license to evil. The real problem with what was done to people of African descent was that those devising policies and those in control of the system believed this was mandated unto them by something called "Manifest Destiny".

They believed so strongly in "Manifest Destiny that they wrote in the founding documents; "We hold these truths to be self-evident that all men are created equal" while stating that being Black meant you were "three-fifths human" and nothing more than property. This system was intended to use and abuse people in a fashion unmatched since the days of Roman oppression. Then, they prayed and asked God to Bless America.

The desperate starving settlers; the helplessness of the displaced Africans; the lure of enormous profits for the slave traders and planters; the required superior status for whites; the immoral and elaborate controls through legal and social punishment up to and including murder - made it work. These were the complex tools of oppression that would be a staple for the white aristocrats holding power. It is important to note that these settlers were those Europeans whose governments, in most cases, wanted to rid themselves of and labeled misfits, rogues, vagabonds, and the more dangerous religious zealots.

Slavery legally ended in excess of 140 years ago. However, as a result of the more than 300 years that African American's experienced its brutality and unnaturalness, it is clear to me that the effects of this continue to affect the psychology of African American to this very day. Because of the effects of this system and through natural life processes the current generation of African Americans, though many generations removed from the actual experience of slavery, still carry the scars of this experience, both socially and mentally. So I say "the system was designed to protect the system" and it continues to work effectively.

I think the great scholar, Dr. Carter G. Woodson, the man responsible for what we know today as Black History Month said it best: "*If you can control a man is thinking you don't have to worry about his actions.*" It is very important to remember Boo that we have survived because we remained free in our minds. As I looked at him with his face full of horror; I'm not sure if he understood what I was saying but like my Grandfather did with me, I knew he was hearing me and it was being stored in his conciseness to be retrieved in the future.

Chapter Five

My grandson is a cartoon fanatic. I guess it's the animation aspect of this medium that intrigues his young mind and causes him to experience a certain level of creativity. Although I must admit, the cartoons of today are not like the cartoons I watched as a child. We only had three channels with cartoons primarily on Saturday mornings and maybe an hour in the afternoon each day. Today's kids have 8 to 10 channels devoted to just cartoons twenty four hours a day. With that said, we started our day with the remote in hand.

I asked him "what channel do you want to watch?" To my surprise he said, "I don't want to watch cartoons. I want you to tell me more stories". With a warm smile I reminded him that a story is most often not true. What I'd been saying was not a fairy tale. It was true and it really happened. I was so happy that he was interested in this truth. I knew this part of history would never be taught to him in a classroom. Instead, he would spend many years being brainwashed with the concept of the American Dream that was being taught through the education process. I know, because I was conditioned that way.

I turned on the television and there was a newscaster standing in front of the White House talking about the election. Boo asked, "Granddad can we go there today so I can see where President Obama is going to live"? Since we lived just a short distance from DC I responded like any grandfather. "We must first have breakfast, get dressed and yes we can go". He took me by the hand pulling me out of bed in a very excited manner rushing me as if we were going to Disney World or something. We quickly ate a bowl of cereal, got dressed, and off we went downtown to visit the White House.

I thought it would be fun if we caught the subway, which we call the Metro, because I knew he had never ridden the rail. I thought doing so would add a little more excitement to the experience. We enjoyed the ride which, surprisingly, was not too crowded but was filled with the euphoria of the day. As we headed to our destination I took the opportunity to continue talking about the amazing event of the day.

After boarding the subway I noticed an older white man sitting near us smiling at my grandson. He reached for Boo's hand to shake it and said, "Young man you can now live". I was stunned by the remark. So I ask the man, "What do you mean?" But, before he could answer I asked, "Are you talking about Mr. Obama being President?" He looked at me and said, "Yes Sir." Then he looked at my grandson with compassion and said, "Today the medicine of all your pain, suffering, and injustice has been corrected".

I looked at the gentleman knowing this was a positive gesture or maybe even a release of guilt. Then he added, "Your life and, particularly that of the boy's, has changed more than you can imagine." I was somewhat surprised by his use of the word "boy" but I understood the mentality of supremacy would not change in the blink of an eye. The old guy then gave me a firm handshake and exited at the next stop. Boo and I got off two stops later at the nearest station to the White House about three blocks away.

It was a slightly brisk day as we walked hand in hand across Lafayette Park toward the blocked off section of 1600 Pennsylvania Avenue in front of the White House. The feeling was so exhilarating that many people mingled about the area as if they wanted the current president to leave now. To the shock of a group near us as we approached the White House, I asked my grandson to salute the current president. This was not done as a show of support, rather as a thank you.

You see, this guy was almost universally considered the worst president of all who came before him. The salute was to say his administration was so inept, causing the country to be in such a pathetic state that America elected a Negro as president. Thank you "W"! This guy left our people in New Orleans to drown, started two wars, caused a financial meltdown, and as a matter of fact should not have been president in the first place.

While walking through the park with the White House in clear view I began to tell my grandson the history of this place. "Boo, as America moved to a more formal and permanent government the enslaved Africans built these magnificent structures that became symbols of opulence, representing the American government, e.g., the Capital and the White House to name a few."

It is a fact that Washington planner, Pierre L'Enfant, rented slaves from nearby owners to dig the foundation for the White House, not paying the slaves rather paying their owners for the work they did. There were others like White House designer James Hoben who used some of his slaves as carpenters to build this structure. From the very beginning, the men and women in bondage not only built but served America's presidents and first families.

The very first President, George Washington, the so-called "Father of the Country", forced slaves from Mount Vernon to work as staff inside "the President's House" in Philadelphia during his term. Thus began a tradition of enslaved men and women working for the president in his residence; a practice that continued until the 1850's. So you see it is important that you understand that black workers made the White House function and to this very day they are an important part of its daily operations.

History never valued people of African descent for anything more than what they were - slave labor. Not only did they work in the White House but enslaved men and women lived there as well. According to the White House Historical Association, the slave and servant quarters were in the basement - now the ground floor. Those rooms now include the library, china room, offices, the formal Diplomatic Reception Room and who knows what else.

The first child born in the White House was the grandson of President Thomas Jefferson. Now, Boo I am going to tell you the most unknown fact in all of American history. The first African American baby born in the White House occurred in 1806 to Fanny and Eddy, two of Jefferson's slaves and his property. This child was also considered a slave by virtue of his parents being owned by the then president. However, some have suggested that this child may have been Jefferson's. Unfortunately, the child would not live beyond the age of two.

The first tale of White House life was written by someone who lived there, Paul Jennings, President James Madison's personal slave, who debunked many myths in his memoirs; such as, the often repeated White House legend of first lady Dolley Madison saving the famous portrait of George Washington from the invading British troops. According to Jennings this was "totally false". He said, "She had no time for doing it. It would have required a ladder to get it down. All she carried off was the silver."

Instead a Frenchman, John Suse and Magraw, the president's gardener, took the painting down and sent it off on a wagon. So you see Boo, His-Story more often than not is a lie. Jennings, who had been a slave working for the Madison's showed the engrained compassion within our people when he gave part of the money he earned as a freedman to help a destitute Dolley Madison after her husband's death.

Years later, African Americans moved from slaves to honored guests. President Andrew Johnson appointed William Slade as the first White House steward, the person charged with running the domestic side of the White House. President Abraham Lincoln met with abolitionists Frederick Douglass and Sojourner Truth in the White House. As you can imagine, the progress was hardly smooth or welcomed as far as being invited as a citizen.

Years later, President Theodore Roosevelt formally invited Booker T. Washington to the White House for dinner. The Southern newspapers were so outraged that they publicly condemned Roosevelt after they learned of the invitation. He never invited another African American to a White House dinner. All the while behind the scenes African American domestic workers kept the White House humming along.

When the first war bonds were issued in April 1942 President Roosevelt did a little presale publicity using an African America to launch the campaign. The first person to whom he sold a war bond to was John Pye who had loyally worked at the White House for the sum of $18.75 a year. This was another example of compassion and patriotism of a near slave to show his love and loyalty to a country that had been so unfair. This was a man who was not allowed to share the same public facilities during segregation. Yet, he loved this country so much that he invested what little he had in it.

Not only did blacks work in the White House, they eventually started working as employees at the White House. E. Frederick Morrow was the first African American appointed as a White House aide by Eisenhower nearly two hundred years after it was built by slaves. John F. Kennedy named Andrew Hatcher associate press secretary in 1960. Despite these few very small steps and their contributions, blacks experienced as much racism inside the White House as they did in the segregated society at large.

And now, two hundred and some odd years later, Barack Obama's election means he will live in the White House as the 44th president. He will be the first black chief executive and the most powerful man in the world. Our journey as African Americans, long and difficult, has brought us to this day. Despite the complicated and disparaging history of African Americans in America; the last vestige of the "White Only" signs will have been removed on the day that Barack Obama moves in as President of the United States.

Chapter Six

We took a few pictures for posterity at the gates of the White House with the hope that my grandson would always remember this day. Since we were already downtown I thought going over to the National Mall would be a good way to finish the day. If you don't know, the Mall is where Dr. King gave the famous "I have a Dream Speech". So we caught the subway and headed for the mall. Throughout the day there was a never before known feeling of jubilation present with everyone we encountered. I won't go so far as to call it a glow but something did radiate and it filled the air.

We exited the subway in the middle of the Mall where we were able to see all the grand structures of opulence; the monument, the museums, and of course the Capital building where Mr. Obama, number 44, would take the oath of office. We found us a spot with a clear view of the entire Mall while I continued to tell to my grandson about those times that came before us.

Boo seemed focused and fascinated. He wanted to know and understand the relevance of this remarkable day. Actually, I was enjoying this experience as much as my grandson. It might even be fair to say I was proud to be able to put into perspective the enormous significance of the day. I was still numb but very aware that I'd been so blessed to witness what most thought to be impossible. To be honest, I'd passed and seen the Capital a million times but on this day it looked brighter and more all-encompassing than ever before.

I wanted to empower my grandson in the oral African tradition of storytelling about this place known to locals as the Federal Triangle. Prior to establishing the nation's capital in Washington DC, the Congress and its predecessors met in Philadelphia, New York City and in a number of other locations. In September 1774, the First Continental Congress brought together delegates from all of the colonies followed by the Second Continental Congress that met from 1775 to 1781.

It was around 1776, when certain important people in the English colonies made a discovery that would prove enormously useful for the next two hundred years. They realized by creating a nation, a legal entity called the United States they could take over land, profit, and political power from the aristocrats of the British Empire. These men realized they could also repel a number of potential rebellions between the poor whites, slaves, and the Indians. The idea was to create a consensus of popular support for the rule of a new privileged leadership, in other words the "Founding Fathers".

It was brilliant when you think about the American Revolution and what was achieved. The colonies had no army or means to defeat the British, which at the time was the most powerful empire on earth. It was said at the time that "it was so vast that the sun never set on the Empire". They only had their will to achieve independence for themselves. So they convinced the populists to join the elite who conjured up this notion to break away from England. The populists and settlers, who did not own property and therefore had few rights or privileges, were persuaded to fight for their freedom given only the promise of land and rights if they fought. It didn't matter to the elite who fought.

They recruited men from all walks of life; the poor, indigent, servants, and slaves - all under the guise of freedom. Yes, I said slaves. Many slaves and people of African descent fought for the cause with the illusion of freedom that waited at the war's conclusion, which of course, they never received. This was a proposition that hugely benefited the elite because those that fought had at best a fifty-fifty chance of returning from the war to collect what was promised. Those who did return, more often than not, didn't receive what they were promised. If they were able to collect, they were taxed and treated in the same manner in which they were before the promised freedom.

So from the very beginning, it was not about the disenfranchised people of the population who sacrificed real blood for America as patriots. It could be argued that this was the greatest robbery of all times because these very clever men stole a country. Now, giving credit where credit is due, the Founding Fathers deserve the highest praise for this enormous feat that showed future generations of leadership the advantages of combining paternalism with command. When people speak of the Constitution and the Founding Fathers with such reverence it is evidence that the model still works effectively today.

What is not often spoken is that there was unrest from the very beginning by the populists. For example there was an incident in June 1783, which was just one of many rebellions that had to be put down. The new Congress seeking protection from an angry mob at a Philadelphia meeting asked the governor of Pennsylvania to call up the militia to protect them from attacks by protesters. History records this event as the "Pennsylvania Mutiny of 1793". However, the governor sympathized with the protesters and refused to remove the mob. As a result, Congress was forced to flee to Princeton, New Jersey before meeting in Annapolis and then fleeing to Trenton - ending up in New York.

The government body that occupied the Capital was established upon ratification of the Constitution in 1789 and New York City remained its home until 1790. At which time the Residence Act was passed to pave way for a permanent capital. The decision to locate the capital was contentious but Alexander Hamilton helped broker a compromise in which the Federal government would take on war debt incurred during the Revolutionary War in exchange for support from northern states for locating the capital along the Potomac River. As part of the legislation, Philadelphia was chosen as a temporary capital for ten years until the nation's capital in Washington DC would be ready.

The design of the Capital building was submitted by James Diamond, one of many submitted in the 1792 contest, but not selected. Pierre Charles L'Enfant was tasked with creating the city plan for the new capital, which was to cover ten square miles. It is also important to note that the man who surveyed the city of Washington DC was a black man - Benjamin Banneker. When it was time to build L'Enfant chose Jenkins Hill as the site for the Capitol Building with a grand boulevard connecting it with the President's House and a public space stretching westward to the Potomac River.

In reviewing L'Enfant's plan Thomas Jefferson insisted the legislative building be called the "Capitol" rather than "Congress House". The word "Capitol" comes from the Latin word meaning city on a hill. In addition to coming up with a city plan L'Enfant had been tasked with designing the Capitol and President's House but he was let go in February 1792 over disagreements with George Washington and the commissioners. There were no plans at that point for the Capitol. What was interesting was the cost of the project - a mere $500. Well, my grandson upon hearing five hundred dollars said, "That's all." I had to smile because Boo was thinking in today's money and did not realize that slaves were the labor, which meant labor cost was virtually zero.

The entire length of the Mall area is about eighteen to twenty blocks and on this brisk day my grandson and I walked the entire length. I gave him a grand tour of the center of world power and the foundations of what I sometimes refer to as the hypocrisy of democracy. By that I mean, the Founding Fathers owned slaves, displaced their families, raped and fathered children with their slaves, denied them rights and passed laws to ensure that Blacks remained in bondage as chattel. These were men claiming to seek freedom but in all honesty they were just hypocrites.

When we finally reached the Washington Monument I was beat but the euphoria of the day kept me going. Most people think the Monument was named after the city of Washington - not true. It was name after George Washington. In fact, the corner stone laid on July 4, 1848 was the same trowel used when George Washington laid the cornerstone of the Capitol in 1793. Of course, this bright eyed little boy wanted to go to the top of it and of course I agreed. We entered and began the slow rise to the top of the 555 foot structure that my grandson called "the great pencil" because of its shape.

I'll admit to being a bit uncomfortable once we reached the top. Nonetheless, I took great pleasure in eagerly pointing out the many monuments and significant locations around the city. The "Great Pencil" without a doubt, offers the best view of the most amazing city in the world - spectacular. One of the things that make grandparents so special is that we are tasked with the ability to create lasting memories. I know this day will be one that Boo will never forget. This was the perfect complement to a day when the world changed forever.

I wanted to teach him, like my grandfather taught me, "If you don't know where you came from - you will never know where you're going". It's been said that knowledge is power. I say, having knowledge and knowing how to use it gives you power. For some reason I felt the need to expound upon that by saying "live your life forward and remember to review it backward because the world has changed forever". What a great feeling spending this historic day with my grandson. PRICELESS!

Chapter Seven

My grandfather was the most important person in my life, which added to the great feeling of being blessed to have a grandson as wonderful as Boo, especially during this epic moment in time. When I was a child my Granddaddy would talk to me or maybe I should say he talked, I listened. He would call that "learning me". I find that ironic because I am now Granddad and doing the same thing with my grandson. My Granddaddy would tell me that "I raised you to be a man. You don't know what you might have to do as a man but when the time comes – just do it". I must impress this powerful testament upon Boo as he writes his life's story.

My grandfather was a sharecropper and lived a hard life as a result of the rigid era of Jim Crow. Maybe this was what made him such a strong, wise man. He would tell me to beware of what I see because things are not always as they seem. It was hard to understand some of what he told me as a youngster but I believed what he told me knowing that he used his wisdom to empower me. I lived with him and grew up on a farm where he was a tenant famer for over fifty years. Actually, that is a polite way of saying near slave. As a tobacco farmer there was something called the stripping season. Granddaddy would use that time, among others, to "learn me".

Let me explain, once the tobacco was harvested and hung in the barn, it took several months to cure. The next step in the process was to completely strip each leaf from the plant. This would take place in the late fall and early winter and it was the most boring dirty job in the world. It was done, usually in a cellar, a damp dirty room submerged in a corner of the barn. It was used to avoid the cool or cold weather. It also doubled as a playhouse or a hiding place for us during the off-season.

Stripping was a tedious process done day in and day out for months. Needless to say, I hated it but as a captive audience, Granddaddy had a lot of time to talk to me and use the old cellar as a classroom. It was during this time that Granddaddy introduced me to the concept of dreams and the importance of having one. He would say, "How can you want something if you don't know what it is that you want. Knowing what you want is the essence of having a dream." He would add that a dream is nothing if you don't have the resilience to make it a reality.

My Granddaddy would tell me that those who dream by day are planning for things that escape those who dream only at night. This was how my education of life and manhood began. There was one story in particular that stood out more than any other. This tale had the most profound and lasting impact of all of those life lessons and I take every opportunity to share this with Boo as often as I can. I am sure my grandson wonders why I keep telling this story much in the way I did a long time ago. It may take time for him to completely understand but as my Granddaddy would say, "If you hear me, not just listen to me, you will inherit life's goodness".

This very important lesson involved his friend Bob. A man who I thought was a little strange or maybe even crazy. Well, crazy is a bit strong but the message contained in the story held a powerful lesson. The way Granddaddy would tell the story; Mr. Bob's job was to offer a prayer every Sunday morning at church during the service prior to the preacher's sermon, a job he had held for years. Sunday was a special day for the community and for him to have a position where he would have the attention of everyone was a big deal. More accurately stated it was a platform for him to perform. He would have been a great entertainer - I had been a witness to this many times.

Mr. Bob would walk to church every Sunday morning, rain or shine, from his home. The trip was several miles up and down hills and around curves. The old guy would be dressed in his best suit, which may have been his only suit, for the morning service. During the walk he would practice his part for the service, the prayer, with the intention of making it a show complete with screams and tears. This show would sometimes last thirty minutes. There were many Sundays that I would wonder how one man could have so much to ask of the Lord. I would think, please, let somebody else get a blessing.

On his way to church this particular Sunday Mr. Bob came across an injured snake. In what he perceived as divine intervention God said to him help this poor creature. He realized he did not have a prayer for that day's service, so he thought, if I help the snake I can pray for us to have the strength to help all of God's creatures. Since the snake is the lowliest of all creatures this would really inspire the congregation and hopefully give them the encouragement to do the same - at least until next Sunday's message. So he picked up the badly injured snake and placed him in a safe place until he could return from church.

With great energy and now inspired, Mr. Bob went on his way. He planned and practiced his prayer as he marched on to church. After he arrived and exchanged a few greetings the service began with a joyful noise, as they say, meaning full of song. Then it was his turn to pray. He began to pray with a powerful tone full of emotion. He asked God to give each person within the sound of his voice the strength to reach out and help all God's creatures from the loving dove to the lowly snake. His message had many in the tiny church standing with shouts of Amen. He felt he had done his job as he closed, asking God to bless the church and said Amen. In his usual style this took about a half hour.

To his surprise, the pastor chose a sermon nearly identical to his message, which took about another hour and a half, talking about helping all of God's creatures. What a great day it was Mr. Bob thought. Normally after the service ended everyone hung around and fellowshipped as it was one of the few chances they had to socialize. Mr. Bob would not hang around on this day - he had a mission and left church in a hurry. He rushed back to the spot where his injured snake was placed hoping it would still be there. He was very excited when he arrived to find it was where he left it. He put his snake in a burlap bag he had gotten from the church and took the snake home.

Over the next several weeks Mr. Bob cared for this creature, desperately trying to save the snake, eventually nursing it back to health. About three weeks later, he thought it was time to take his snake back to where he found it, thinking it was well enough to be set free. The following Sunday, he put on his best suit and started his journey to church with snake in hand. As he arrived at the spot where he had found the snake; he thought what a wonderful thing he had done. He was sure to receive God's blessing for this act of kindness.

He rubbed the snake gently and said goodbye. However, as he reached into the bag to grab it, the snake raised his head and bit him. Then bit him again and again. Mr. Bob cried out, why would you bite me after all I've done for you? My God why? I guess he was expecting an answer from God but none came. He repeated his cry once more. Then the snake stuck his head out of the bag and said, "I am a snake and that's what we do."

I heard this story over and over again for years. In fact, it took years for me to figure out the message concealed within the story. It was a lesson that would prove to be invaluable as I journeyed through life. The moral of the story was this: "be careful in your dealings with people because people, just like the snake, will hurt you - that's what they do." These and other stories like this had a positive impact on my development and it was my duty to pass these lessons on to my grandson.

My Granddaddy would say things like "God bless the child that's got his own." He constantly reminded me that everything that ever was came from a single thought and if you can think it; you can figure out how to do it - just put your mind to it. I would constantly hear him say "a man must be able to do what needs to be done when it needs to be done regardless of the circumstances". Therefore, I am compelled to teach my grandson that the difference between a man and a boy is the lessons he's learned.

I found myself telling Boo that you will always have enemies. Your enemy is anyone who attempts to sabotage the assignment God has for your life. Your enemy is anybody who may resent you for doing positive things and will be unhappy because of your success. These people will attempt to kill the faith that God has breathed within you. They would rather discuss your past than your future because they don't want you to have one. Your enemy should not be feared and it is important to understand that this person usually will be closest person to you. Granddaddy would tell me to use them as bridges, not barricades.

It is important that my grandson understand that there is no such thing as luck. The harder you work at something the luckier you get. Luck is only preparation meeting opportunity. I could tell the way he looked at me that it would require some thinking on my part to figure out the messages within the lesson. For example, life is all about survival and if you are to survive - never bring a knife to a gunfight. This would be just as foolish as using a shotgun to kill a mosquito. He must also know that it is not the size of the dog in the fight; it is the size of the fight in the dog.

I would tell him to always take the road less traveled, make your own path but be sure to leave a trail for others to follow. Life's road is often hard; just make sure you travel it wisely. If you have a thousand miles to go, you must start the journey with the first step. I remembered one of Granddaddy's favorite humorous sayings that I often share with Boo. "Moses started out as a basket case." Please understand that hard times will come and when they come, do not drown in your tears, always swim in your blessings.

As I proudly looked at my grandson I said, "I have told you about history that was not fair or just but historians would have you believe differently. His-Story paints a picture that is simply not true, for the most part, particularly when it comes to that of African Americans." If history could erase that which I had witnessed and know to be true; how can you trust anything history told as truth? Do not always believe what you are told. Research, get another opinion, and determine for yourself because nothing is as it seems.

My goal was to firmly plant the seeds and ensure that my grandson knows that he could do common things in life in an uncommon way - and by doing so he would command the attention of the world. After all, he could grow up to be president, if he wanted, as long as he remembered that life is not a rehearsal. It's real and it is he who will create his destiny if he did not allow others to control it. In the strongest voice that I could conjure I would say to him, "can't is not a word. Never use it because it implies failure. It is also smart to stay away from those who do use it."

When I look at Boo, I see his father's eyes and think about the pain of losing my son. Therefore, I cherish the fact that Jarad left him with me because as he is the most precious gift anyone could be given. It was very important and necessary to tell him just how special he is to me. "Boo you are an important creation and God gave you to us as a special gift for the purpose of changing the world".

It may be hard sometimes, you may not understand, you may have self-doubt or hesitation but never quit. You must promise me Boo that you will never give up. Then, I will rest knowing that I may not be the one to change the world but I have gifted the knowledge and shared it with the mind that will change it.

Chapter Eight

I continued to impress upon my grandson's young mind that people will walk in and out of your life, like history, with both ever changing. Moreover, he must know that these memories, like our bond, will leave a huge footprint upon his heart forever to which I am simply blessed to share. Frankly, I believe his young life was assigned to me for the purpose of enrichment or as my Granddaddy would say "to dictate the rhythm of his soul".

If my knowledge can empower my grandson, and it will, he will know the value of life and grow into greatness. It is very important that he use his head, which means the right stuff needs to be put in it if he is to successfully navigate the journey of his life. This wisdom will allow him to follow his heart in order to reach his destination. I've always believed that great minds discuss ideas; average minds discuss events and small minds discuss people. In other words, it is necessary for him to control his emotions and use logic in order to survive.

This is very important because he is part of this new generation that lacks direction and clarity; the now generation. Therefore, I must teach him that a person, who loses money, loses much but the person who loses a friend loses much more. I want my grandson to know, in no uncertain terms, "that if he's alone; I will be his shadow. If he wants to cry, I will be the shoulder to lean on. If he needs a hug, my shoulder will be the pillow and I will hold him tightly. When he searches for happiness, he will always find my smile and when he needs me - I'll always be here."

When we finally reached the subway and boarded it. Boo immediately fell asleep. While holding him in my arms my mind went back to how this all began and by that I mean this grand experiment called the Democracy. It was devised with the idea of a legacy based upon dependency, apathy, and the entrenchment of an American social order. If you know His-Story, it provides clear evidence of its diabolical intent to bankrupt the souls of African Americans based on this ideology of supremacy.

There are many stolen souls that still reside within our community who bear the burden of a system that perpetrated, in the name of God, mankind's greatest crime. What they did was physically take an entire race of people, erased their culture and brutally corrupted their minds by removing any possibility of knowing who they were, which prevents them from knowing who they are today. Therefore, from the beginning, people of African descent were intended to be a nation living within a nation without a nationality.

Surely with the election of a man, who looks like us, as president, if for no other reason, than to educate our people about the many issues that people of African descent continue to face; as a result of the untreated wounds inflicted by America's forefathers that have caused discord that still reigns in the African American Diaspora. Therefore, I feel that if I empower my grandson with this knowledge these through truths and this factual examination of our past. He will then understand the root cause of the asymptomatic behaviors that endure within our community.

It is my sincere desire to help him understand that there is a conditioning in certain communities, which is not an excuse, rather an explanation as to why these behaviors were never unlearned and have been passed down from generation to generation. When I reexamine my relatively short lifetime I have been referred to as Colored, Negro, Afro-American, Black, and an African American, which were all polite terms assigned to make known that as a person of color I was not a true American citizen. This is important for him to understand.

Although African Americans are no longer slaves physically; a mental enslavement remains that is as old as the nation itself. The institution of slavery was designed to deprive a people of their God given rights through sustained policies of control. To overcome these indignities we must realize that education is the single most important ingredient necessary to neutralize the forces that breed poverty and despair. Regardless of how much we were, and are held down, it is my responsibility through this teaching, to help him find a way to get up; even if the system is designed to keep him down.

There is an old proverb that says "learning without thought is a labor lost; thought without learning is intellectual death". To fully understand this thought my grandson must know that courage is knowing what is needed and then doing it. As tenacious beings we must understand that there is no such thing as an inferior mind. So, I say it's time for an awakening. If for no other reason than to honor those who sacrificed so much in order for us to live life in abundance.

As my mind revisited the past I was reminded of a college course I once taught. The required text for the class was "*The Mis-Education of the Negro*"; the most profound novel ever written in my opinion. It was an amazing experience because of the powerful messages revealed within the pages. Especially when you consider this great literary work was originally published in 1933 by Dr. Carter G. Woodson who is known as the father of Black History Month. This book should be mandatory reading for all African Americans.

The thesis of Dr. Woodson's book is that Negroes of his day were being culturally indoctrinated rather than taught in American schools and not given the advantage of education. This conditioning, he claims, causes African Americans to become dependent seeking out inferior places in the greater society of which they are a part. This assertion is clearly evident nearly eighty years later. Therefore, looking at the mental state of Black America we have not understood the potent message left for us.

He challenged his readers to become empowered by doing for themselves regardless of what they were taught: *"History shows that it does not matter who is in power... those who have not learned to do for themselves and have to depend solely on others never obtain any more rights or privileges in the end than they did in the beginning."* We must pray that this will not be the case with regard to the new president.

We are a unique people, a forgiving people, a steadfast people, and a brave people unlike any known to the world. It was our labor that built this country and in large part responsible for the great wealth America enjoys to this very today. We cannot expect others and particularly those in power to address our survival need. When you look upon America's enormous wealth and the power people of African American decent have produced for the benefit of the other hue; it is unbelievable that the tremendous control of resources has never been shared with us.

We have looked out for this country for hundreds of years and are still doing so today, which is simply amazing and deserving of honor. Today, with all the advantages concerning educational opportunities, business exposure, social networking and now the first African American President we are in the best position to succeed than at any time in our history. So the question is "why are we not?"

Every other ethnic community takes advantage of these options to strengthen and empower their communities while robbing our communities in the process. We will let anybody set up shop in our communities and take our money. There is another profound proverb that we should adopt which says "if you want to go quickly go it alone but if you want to far go together".

My point is: We must learn to do business with each other in order to gain wealth by keeping our money in our communities. Some say we spend a trillion dollars annually and nearly all of it leaves our community within 15 minutes. With that said, the definition of insanity is to continue to do the same things and expect different results. We can change the world but first we must change ourselves.

I am reminded of another famous quote from "The Mis-Education of the Negro": *"When you control a man's thinking you do not have to worry about his actions. You do not have to tell him not to stand here or go yonder. He will find his 'proper place' and will stay in it. You do not need to send him to the back door. He will go without being told. In fact, if there is no back door, he will cut one for his special benefit. His education makes it necessary."* This phrase speaks to what was used to divide an entire race of people.

While looking at my grandson sleeping soundly I thought why haven't we built upon what was left for us to survive? Trust and believe thoughts are things and you are only what you think. Therefore, it was my charge to design and be the author of his story with the main premise being "know where you came from in order to know where you're going".

My grandson must realize that the power within him is greater than the power outside of him and that his mind is capable of endless expectations and unlimited possibilities. I do not want my grandson to place that power and trust in the hands of a system that has historically oppressed or worse continue to oppress our people.

Chapter Nine

The sun began to slowly set on the amazing day and I really didn't want it to end. But it had been a very long day with lots of walking and both of us were drained. However, it was the euphoric feeling in the air that, without question, made this day one of the most incredible days of my life. Possibly, because I could see the twinkle in Boo's eyes that seemed to hold a certain promise that I had never known. It was the feeling of knowing that I had lived long enough to realize that the souls of our people could be made whole.

At the end of a short subway ride I knew we could not end such an amazing day without doing another one of our favorite things - a stop at the pizza parlor. Yes, like any little boy the lore of McDonalds or pizza was irresistible. Other than a few hot dogs we hadn't eaten much all day. So those mis-meal cramps were attacking both of us. I knew a great spot where we could satisfy those hunger pains. When we entered the establishment I could still feel the exuberance of history. Everyone at every table was excited and talking about the election.

We ordered two pizzas and I continued to talk while we waited for them to arrive. To my surprise, Boo asked me to tell him more about Black History. I was very impressed by his interest and I asked, "What do you know about Black History?" At eight years old, he said the predictable. "I know Rosa Parks, Martin Luther King, Malcolm X, and we have Black History Month". I said, "Boo, African Americans history is rich with great accomplishments but much of it has been never told or recorded."

"You do know that you and I stand on the shoulders of giants". "What do you mean granddad", he asked. Many people gave their lives for us to have life. This is why we celebrate the legacy of Black History Month each year to honor those brave souls who made significant contributions to the benefit of mankind. We have so much to be proud of in spite of the fact that most of our history was stolen or erased.

This is why we must appreciate this month dedicated to educating and paying homage to tremendous contributions people of color have made to the world. I am blessed to have lived long enough to witness what no one living or dead ever thought was possible, the election of the first African American President of these United States and the leader of the free world. It is the most significant historical event since the resurrection of Christ.

This is not withstanding all of the storied achievements made by the ghosts of the greats who blazed mighty trails. As proud as I am of the many contributions African Americans have made to this great country, and to the world, I am equally as confident that there is an abundance of history yet to be made. Let me tell you about the origins of Black History Month? "Yes, granddad", he replied.

The idea of Black History Month was conceived in Chicago during the summer of 1915. An alumnus of the University of Chicago with many friends in the city hosted a convention where Dr. Carter G. Woodson traveled from Washington DC to participate. It was a national celebration of the fiftieth anniversary of the emancipation of slavery sponsored by the State of Illinois. "Emancipation is a big word granddad. What does it mean?" I smiled and told him that "it is supposed to mean freedom".

Thousands of African Americans traveled from all across the country that summer to see exhibits highlighting the progress African Americans had made since the extermination of slavery. Awarded a doctorate at Harvard three years earlier, Dr. Woodson joined other exhibitors with a black history display. He was so enamored with the idea that he began the process of making this exhibit an annual event, which means we owe the celebration of Black History month to Dr. Woodson.

In 1924, his group responded with the creation of Negro History and Literature Week, which they renamed Negro Achievement Week. Their outreach was significant but Dr. Woodson desired a greater impact. He told students at the Hampton Institute, "We are going back to that beautiful history and it is going to inspire us to greater achievements." In 1925, he decided that the Association had to shoulder the responsibility. He felt going forward with this idea would both create and popularize knowledge about black history.

He sent out a press release announcing Negro History Week in February of 1926. Dr. Woodson chose the second week of February because it marked the birthdays of two Americans who greatly influenced the lives and social condition of African Americans: Abraham Lincoln and former slave Frederick Douglass. It is a myth that the month of February was selected because it is the shortest month; it is simply not true.

Dr. Woodson also founded the Association for the Study of Negro Life and History, which is now the Association for the Study of African American Life and History. What you might not know is that black history had barely begun to be studied or even documented when the tradition originated.

As my grandson looked on with wide eyes I reminded him that blacks have been in America since August of 1619. When a Dutch man-of-war ship rode the tide into Jamestown, Virginia and the first slaves were dragged onto its shores. Yet, it was not until the 20th century that African American history gained limited presence in any history books.

From the beginning, Dr. Woodson was overwhelmed by the response to his call. Negro History Week appeared across the country in schools and in many public forums. The expanding black middle class became participants in and consumers of black literature and culture. Black history clubs sprang up, teachers demanded materials to instruct their pupils, and progressive whites supported their efforts. They set a theme for the annual celebration providing study materials such as pictures, lessons for teachers, plays for historical performances, and posters of important dates and people.

The shift to a month-long celebration began even before Dr. Woodson's death. As early as the 1940's, blacks in West Virginia, a state where Dr. Woodson often spoke, began to celebrate February as Negro History Month. The 1960's had a dramatic effect on the study and celebration of black history. Before the decade was over Negro History Week would be well on its way to becoming Black History Month.

This was the result of young blacks on college campuses in the 1960's who became increasingly conscious of their links to Africa. These young intellectuals, part of the awakening, prodded Woodson's organization to change with the times. They succeeded in 1976 fifty years after the first celebration. The Association used its influence to institutionalize the shifts from a week to a month and from Negro history to black history.

Since then, every American President, Democrat and Republican, has issued proclamations endorsing the Association's annual theme because Black History is American History. Boo, never ever forget the profound legacy of our past nor fail to embrace it with pride. We are defined by our honor and redeemed by our pride and as such, we are merely the sum of the whole.

Chapter Ten

The pizza was really good. Then, we started the short ride home. Boo quickly fell asleep and slept like a lamb the entire trip. I like that metaphor because I often refer to him as my precious Lamb of God. When we reached the house I carried him inside thinking I would tuck him in for the night. But he was awakened by the news as I watched TV. As happy as I was, I was not surprised to see the reality of the event had now caused some to spout the kind of vitriol that said racism had raised its ugly head. I could now see that everyone was not as excited as I was.

Boo was still thirsting for knowledge and asked if I would tell him a bedtime story. I asked, "What story do you want me to tell you?" I thought he might want to hear something like "The Three Bear or Billy Goat Gruff." He quickly said, "Oh no Granddad, I want you to tell me more stories about black people." I had to laugh at his response although I was very proud of what he said. We had had a long day and I was dead tired. So I promised him that tomorrow, "I will tell you about black people starting at the beginning".

Sure enough as soon as he woke up - "You ready to learn me granddad". I was taken aback by that because he remembered that's what my Granddaddy used to say to me. I got him a bowl of cereal and a cup of coffee for myself as we were now seated at the kitchen table. First, I want you to know that we were the first people to have thought and to walk the earth. With that said, in the oral tradition of those who came before us, I began the journey back in time.

Long – long ago there was a place where history tells us mankind was born. This place of magnificent splendor was known as Pangaea. Back then it consumed all of the earth's land mass and it was the birthplace of civilization. This place has evolved to what we know today as Africa. During its evolution there have been many tribes, nations, countries, and cultures to dot its landscape. By virtue of its wealth and many civilizations of great stature, the continent has altered the course of the world.

The history of the black man is the oldest and the least known of all mankind. The continuing study of our past indicates that central Africa bears evidence of being the land of the first human life. It is on the continent of Africa that the oldest human-like fossils have been found. In fact, the oldest human like remains found was given the name "Lucy", which is believed to be more than four million years old. So you see Boo, we have been on this little rock called earth for a long time.

There have been many famed archaeologist to unearth human remains nearly two million years old. In fact, they've been able to trace the evolution of man prior to what "His-Story" calls the Old Stone Age. They've also found hand tools such as axes, picks, and even anvils at least fifty thousand years old. In central Nigeria stone tools at least 39,000 years old have been dug from the earth. In addition, they've found many crude calculating devices dating back six thousand years, to include other sensitive relics that survived more than three thousand years.

I want you to know and understand that black men sat on thrones in Egypt at least three thousand years before Christ. There were many African states that existed in the centuries before and after the birth of Christ that were powerful and mighty. It was a Nubian who was the first man to declare the existence of one living God. Actually, African folklore gives us stories very similar to those written in the Bible. "What's a Nubian granddad?" Nubians were black people who controlled the territory from the Mediterranean to the edge of modern Ethiopia.

The African presence in Egypt is still quite noticeable in the statuary which has stared unblinkingly across the centuries. The Sphinx and many other sculptured monuments have the broad nose and full lips of Africans. It is important to note that not only did Africans supply much of the manual labor for the building of the pyramids and the statues of the country; they were the architects and designers of these mighty structures. So you see Boo, Africans did more than roam the jungles as many would have you believe.

They pioneered, along with the Hittites in the making of iron, the working of gold and silver, and in the use of oil-bearing plants for medicinal and dietary purposes, especially palm oil. They developed basic cereals including several kinds of millet and rice. They developed the world's first cotton cloth and developed the art of weaving. The blacks of Africa are believed to have been the world's first farmers, producing wheat, ground nuts, gourds, kola, and possibly coffee and cress, as well as yams, watermelons and peanuts.

While the Europeans were still living in caves, African people were Kings that ruled states. At some point, someone discovered the knowledge of the Nubians and stole that knowledge. They say, and I mean His-Story, that the greatest thinkers the world has ever known hailed from Greece. I would argue that is not true. For example, if you look at some of the paintings and sculptures that reached Greece, Rome, and Europe. It's obvious that they have the influence of Egypt and the Sudan, particularly work in bronze, brass, ivory, quartz and granite.

African influences have been portrayed in the work of Greek sculptors and potters from the beginning of their recorded history. The Greeks were, of course, aware of the color contrast between white and black racial types but there is little to suggest they were particularly concerned with color, as such. A Greek historian, Herodotus, mentioned the presence of Africans in 480 B.C. and wrote of them as "black and curly-haired." There is also ample evidence recorded in history that considerable contact existed between Rome and Africa.

I'm going to take you on an amazing journey that is the greatest story ever told. I'll begin in the year of our Lord 500 AD in a region on the coast of West Africa where there were three mighty empires that flourished. They were the empires of Ghana, Mali, and Songhai each having powerful armies and controlled great wealth that included large quantities of gold, fine manufactured goods, thriving agriculture, and enormous profits from trading.

Their empires' economic strength and centralized political control made it easy to suppress revolts. The rulers of these nations were strong, surrounded by competent loyal government officials, and military commanders who were able to unify empires composed of diverse peoples with different languages, cultures, and geographic locations. The people who inhabited this region were of the Kru, Ashanti, Fante, Ewe, Yoruba, and the Ibo nations to which we are descendants.

The empire of Ghana was founded along the Niger River between the third and fifth centuries. Ghana was established by the Soninke people of West Africa, who quickly developed an economic life comprising agriculture, manufacturing, and international trade. They were superior metal workers and produced iron swords and other weapons used to conquer neighboring peoples while they effectively maintained control over their territory. The empire's growth was relatively slow until Ghana began to trade with Arab ports on the Mediterranean coast and with other kingdoms of East Africa on the Red Sea.

Ghana's ascent to great power was directly related to its acquisition of gold. The name *Ghana* meant "warrior king" used to refer to the empire because of its gold. It was written that Ghana's gold was so abundant that the king's dogs wore gold collars. Al-Bakri, an Arab geographer, wrote that the king owned a nugget of gold so big that he could tether his horse to it. At its height of power Ghana had a functioning judiciary system and other institutions to govern the nation's people. The empire was ruled by a king supported by several provincial governors and viceroys. Ghana dominated the Sudan for three hundred years.

The empire of Mali differed considerably from the Ghana. It became a mighty nation in the seventh century when the small Mandingo state on the upper Niger River was transformed by two great African leaders - Sundiata Keita and Mansa Musa. Although Sundiata Keita began to transform the state into a great empire its growth was slow until Mansa Musa became its ruler.

Mansa Musa, a devout Muslim, set out in 1324 on a pilgrimage to Mecca the holy city for Muslims. His entourage included about sixty thousand persons including twelve thousand servants. As many as five hundred servants each carried a staff of pure gold weighing six pounds.

Eighty camels carried an average of three hundred pounds of gold each. These riches were to be distributed as alms and gifts.

Upon his return from his pilgrimage, Mansa Musa directed his architect to design buildings in Timbuktu and other cities under his control. At times, Mali's empire numbered far more than one hundred thousand people with approximately one-quarter of the population composed of scholars and students. It was a busy place where merchants displayed their merchandise to local and international consumers. Caravans from distant places frequently came to Timbuktu to exchange exotic goods for gold.

Timbuktu is believed to be the first great university rising to its highest level of development during the Songhai's empire between 1493 and 1529. During this time, the University of Timbuktu produced books on subjects ranging from logic, theology, ethics, mathematics, and rhetoric. Akmed Baba was the last chancellor of the university and considered one of the great intellectuals of the sixteenth century establishing a standard unmatched on this earth.

Mali's power derived from strong rulers, a centralized government, and a successful economic base of agriculture, manufacturing, trade, and its amazing wealth in gold. When Mansa Musa died in 1332 the Mali Empire began to disintegrate. Squabbling local rulers could not agree on a central form of government and its neighbors attacked the kingdom's cities. By the mid 1400's, the Mali Empire was decisively destroyed by the sons of the king of Gao. Their revolt set into motion the formation for the Songhai Empire, which inherited a solid economic base from its predecessor. Its growth was substantially accelerated when Askia Mohammed, a general who had been prime minister, gained power in 1493.

In his thirty-six-year quest to make Songhai the most powerful empire in the world, Askia Mohammed embarked on an effort to expand trade to include European countries. He eventually controlled an area of West Africa larger than Europe. The Europeans took notice of its wealth and Askia's greed or naiveté created an inhumane and, dare I say, immoral partnership of destruction with the Europeans. I would argue that this was a pivotal point in the history of our past because it was during his rule that the sale of black slaves became a major business.

Askia was a master politician and a superior leader of people. He restructured the army, secured a system of banking and credit, and established the cities of Gao, Walata, Timbuktu, and Nenne as major intellectual centers where scholarship was encouraged. Timbuktu was a grand city whose stories of intrigue and mystery made it one of the most celebrated cities of its time. It flourished as a business district, a religious site with Great Mosques, and an intellectual center with the University of Sankore.

Although many people of Songhai worked at farming, making tools, weapons, ceremonial items, and artworks of bronze, tin, copper, and gold; the overwhelming majority were warriors. Songhai achieved many military conquests and the empire reached its zenith in the fifteenth and sixteenth centuries. The decline of the Songhai Empire marked the end of the great West African empires and from here the story begins to affect the African American Diaspora.

It appears that at this time the kingdom entered into the slave trade where millions were sold into bondage - never to return. Although, there are others who claim that the collapse came from the collision of two great religions - Islam and Christianity. To that point, with respect to the roles each religion played upon a naive people; it is important to be mindful that there was no word "G-O-D" in any African language before the coming of Europeans nor was there a word "Allah" before the coming of Muslims.

Once this unholy alliance was formed with the Europeans the destruction of an entire race of people was initiated solely out of greed. They captured human beings, their brothers, selling them to the waiting criminals on the coasts. Imagine if you can, being captured, put on a forced march, beaten, put into pins while shackled, and then placed in a tomb-like environment with people you cannot, in many cases, communicate with for months.

These were the conditions leading to that horrible journey for millions of African's forcibly interned into the belly of the beast with their destination unknown. His-Story speaks to this wretched practice as part of the Atlantic Slave Trade. However, we know it as the "Middle Passage", which refers to that middle leg of the transatlantic trade triangle in which millions of Africans were imprisoned, enslaved, and removed forcibly from their place of birth never to return.

The transatlantic trade triangle worked this way. Ships departed Europe for African markets with commercial goods, which were in turn traded for kidnapped Africans who were transported across the Atlantic to be slaves. The enslaved Africans were then sold or traded as commodities for raw materials, which would be transported back to Europe to complete the "triangular trade". A single voyage on the Middle Passage was a large financial undertaking that was generally organized by companies or groups of investors rather than individuals.

African kings, warlords, and private kidnappers sold their captives to Europeans who operated from several coastal forts along the western coast of Africa to await sale to European or American slave traders. A typical slave ship contained several hundred slaves with about thirty crew members. The male captives were chained together in pairs to save space with their right leg chained to the next man's left leg, while the women and children may have had somewhat more room.

The duration of the transatlantic voyage varied widely from one to six months depending on weather conditions. However, it became more efficient over time as the average transatlantic journey of the early 16th century lasted several months. By the 19th century the crossing often required fewer than six weeks. West Central Africa and Southeastern Africa were the most common regions for traders to secure the human cargo that was destined for the Caribbean and the Americas.

The total number of African deaths directly attributable to the Middle Passage is estimated well into the millions. A broader look at African deaths directly attributable to the institution of slavery from 1500 to 1900 suggests up to four million perished but some say the number was close to one third of the Africans captured. It is believed that nearly 60 million were captured. This includes an estimated 15% who died at sea with mortality rates considerably higher in Africa itself during the process of capturing and transporting indigenous peoples to the ships.

What this extraction of captives did was markedly influence the cultural and demographic landscapes of both Africa and the Americas. The Middle Passage has also been said to mark the origin of a distinct African social identity. For example, in America these people came to be known as "Negro", which is a Spanish word that means "Black" but no Spanish country refers to its people of color that way. Another significant point to note was that Europeans did not refer to themselves as "White". They would identify themselves usually by the country they were from until America was born.

For two hundred years Portugal had a quasi-monopoly on the export of slaves from Africa. During the eighteenth century when the slave trade accounted for the transport of about 6 million Africans, the British were responsible for almost 2.5 million of them. Most contemporary historians estimate that between 9 and 12 million Africans arrived in the New World while others remain firm that it was more like one third of the continent's population. Boo, these numbers are staggering and it may be years before you can understand the magnitude of this crime.

Disease and starvation due to the length of the passage were the main contributors to the egregiously high death toll. Then there were the outbreaks of smallpox, syphilis, measles, and other diseases that spread rapidly in the close-quarter compartments. The number of dead increased with the length of the voyage. The incidence of dysentery and scurvy increased with longer stints at sea as the quality and amount of food and water diminished with every passing day.

In addition to physical sickness many slaves became too depressed to eat or function efficiently because of the loss of freedom, family, security, and their own humanity. As you can imagine, the captives were fed as little as possible, actually just enough to keep the cargo alive. They were fed one meal a day with water, usually beans, corn, yams, rice, and palm oil but if food was scarce the slaveholders and the ship's crew would get priority over the slaves.

It is necessary to understand how malicious and cruel the slaver captains were to their human cargo. There was a particular incident known as the Zong Massacre that shows the lengths captains on the passage would go. The Zong was a British slaver that had taken too many slaves on its voyage. The overcrowded ship combined with malnutrition, disease from poor sanitation on the slave decks and living in such close quarters killed several crew members and around 60 slaves.

Bad weather made the Zong's voyage slow and the captain decided to drown his slaves at sea so the owners could collect insurance on the "cargo". More than 100 slaves were killed and a large number chose to kill themselves. I looked at my grandson and saw a tear rolling down his cheek. The pain of this horror affected him hundreds of years after the fact. I continued to explain that a large percentage of all African life loss en-route to America included suicide as well as murder and disease.

Obviously the Zong incident became fuel for the abolitionist movement. A major court case was brought by the slavers but had little success because the insurance company refused to compensate for the loss of the "cargo". While treatment of slaves on the passage varied, the treatment of the human cargo was never good since the captured African men and women were considered less than human. Yes, they were "cargo" and treated as such while being transported for marketing.

History shows that slaves were ill-treated in almost every imaginable manner. While they were generally fed enough to stay alive and given water simply because healthy slaves were more valuable, if resources ran low on the long unpredictable voyages, the crew received preferential treatment. So you see Boo, slave punishment was very harsh because the crew had to turn independent people into obedient slaves. Whipping and the use of the cat o' nine tails were common occurrences. Sometimes they were simply beaten for "melancholy."

Boo asked, "What is a cat o' nine tails"? Well son, it is as whip that is made of nine knotted thongs of cotton cord, about 2 ½ feet, designed to lacerate the skin and cause intense pain. It traditionally has nine thongs as a result of the manner in which rope is plaited. Thinner rope is made from three strands of yarn plaited together, and thicker rope from three strands of thinner rope plaited together. To make a cat o' nine tails, a rope is unraveled into three small ropes, each of which is unraveled again. It had one purpose and that was to inflect pain.

The worst punishments were reserved for rebelling, to which the captains were often horrifically creative. In one instance, a captain punished a failed rebellion by killing one of the slaves involved, immediately, and then forced two other slaves to eat his heart and liver. Slaves resisted their oppressors in a variety of ways. The two most common types of resistance were refusing to eat and the other was suicide. Suicide was a frequent occurrence often by refusal of food and medicine or throwing oneself overboard.

Suicide by jumping overboard was such a problem that captains had to address it directly in many cases. They used the sharks that followed the ships as a terror weapon. One captain who had a rash of suicides on his ship took a woman and lowered her into the water on a rope and then tried to pull her out as fast as possible. But when she came into view the sharks had already killed her by eating the lower half of her body.

Over time certain African people, such as the Kru, came to be thought of as having substandard value as slaves because, they developed a reputation for being too proud for slavery and would attempt suicide immediately upon losing their freedom. Both suicide and self-starvation were prevented as much as possible by slaver crews. In some cases slaves were often force-fed or tortured until they ate; yet some still managed to starve themselves to death.

It was also standard practice to keep slaves away from anything that could help them commit suicide. Often the sides of the deck were netted to prevent the slaves from jumping overboard. It was common when an uprising failed that the mutineers would jump, en masse, into the sea. Interestingly, slaves generally believed if they jumped overboard, they would be returned to their family and friends in their village or join their ancestors in the afterlife.

One account of a slave recorded in a ships log said, "When we found ourselves at last taken away, death was more preferable than life, and a plan was concerted amongst us, that we might burn and blow up the ship, and to perish all together in the flames." The size of the rebellions ran anywhere from a handful of slaves to a large portion of the "cargo". Often the uprisings would end with the death of a few slaves and crew. The remainder were punished or executed at the whim of the captain as an example to the rest of the slaves on board.

Slaves also resisted through certain manifestations of their religions and mythology. They would appeal to their gods for protection asking for vengeance upon their captors and they would also try to curse or otherwise harm the crew using idols and fetishes. One crew found fetishes in their water supply placed by slaves who thought it would kill all who drank from it.

It was not just the slaves who suffered. The sailors themselves experienced terrible conditions and often were employed only through coercion. For example, at port towns recruiters and tavern owners would get sailors very drunk and indebted. They were oftentimes given an offer to relieve their debt if they signed contracts with slave ships. If they did not they would be imprisoned. Sailors in prison had a hard time getting jobs outside of the slave ship industry, since most other maritime industries would not hire "jail-birds," so they were forced to go to the slave ships. As a result, there was usually a portion of the crew who hated the slave trade.

While at sea the sailors faced conditions nearly as harsh as the slaves and their mortality rates were roughly the same. Sailors were also whipped and beaten as punishment, and in an extreme case, a sailor was slowly starved to death chained to a ship's mast because the captain thought he had aided a slave rebellion. The sharks that followed the ships were used, if only passively, to discourage sailors from abandoning the ship. Rarely were crew members relieved of their duty. They usually died in service.

Granddad this is terrible I never learned anything like this in school. "How could people do this to other human beings?" Well son, they said it was done in the name of God. Then my grandson said, "When I go to church, the God that we worship is a good God and would never tell anyone to do bad things like this."

"Believe me it was not true that God told them to do these things. It was evil in the hearts of these repulsive people who placed human being in those ships that rode the tides onto the shores of a place like "merica" where the brutality and horror would continue and worsen for successive lifetimes.

Chapter Eleven

Spending this time with my grandson was truly a blessing. I might add that having the opportunity to share the real history of our people with him during this monumental occasion was more than I could have ever dreamed. I hoped this knowledge would serve as a lasting source of empowerment as I "learned him" by resurrecting this journey through African American History. To be honest, as we witnessed this meaningful occasion of the first black president - I was also empowered.

My goal was to bring into remembrance some of the heart wrenching events and glorious victories resulting from the unimaginable struggles that formed the foundation of the enormous power and strength each of us possess. Maybe Boo would come to realize that these despicable crimes were only matched by what was done to our Lord. Boo was attentively looking at me waiting for the next saga, which was the voyage of no return.

The commodity of human souls was a thoughtfully selected task. It is believed the Africans from Senegal were the most prized items for trade because many were skilled artisans. The most undesirable cargo was the Ibos from Calabar because of their high suicide rate. Accommodations onboard most ships had three decks with the lower two used for transporting slaves. The lowest deck extended the full length of the ship and was no more than five feet high.

The captives were packed into tomb-like compartments side by side to utilize all available space. On the next deck, wooden planks like shelves extended from the sides of the ship where the slaves were chained in pairs at the wrists and ankles crammed side by side. Men occupied middle shelves while women and children were sometimes allowed to move about certain areas of the ship.

There was no sanitation although buckets were provided for use as toilets. However, they were not emptied regularly. The ships smelled of excrement, disease, and death. A typical slave ship coming directly to the American mainland from Africa weighed about one to two hundred tons, although some were slightly larger. Slave ships were eventually built especially for human cargo.

These slave ships could carry as many as four hundred slaves and a crew of forty-seven, as well as thirteen thousand pounds of food. They were long, narrow, fast, and designed to direct air below decks. Shackling irons, nets, and ropes were standard equipment. By the way, the first registered slave ship was named "The Good Ship Jesus," and, in the name of God, these ships sailed the Atlantic full of misery.

As we traveled through time on this expedition through our past, I would be remiss had I not returned to the scene of the crime. By that I mean, the crime scene in America, which would be England's first permanent settlement in North America - the Jamestown Colony. It was a marshy wasteland, poor for agriculture, and a breeding ground for malaria-carrying mosquitoes. The settlement was such a harsh environment that only thirty-two of the estimated one hundred original settlers survived the first seven months. His-Story describes this as the "starving times" but this would soon change.

On August 20, 1619, the first African "settlers" reached North America as cargo onboard a Dutch man-of-war ship that rode the tide onto the shores of this strange place carrying Captain Jope and a cargo of twenty Africans. It is strange that history cannot tell us why this mysterious ship anchored off Jamestown. It is believed the captain needed food and in exchange for food he offered his cargo of Africans as payment.

When the deal was consummated, Antoney, Isabella, and eighteen other Africans disembarked. Although they were not the first Africans to arrive in North America, they were the first African "settlers." Regarded as indentured servants rather than slaves, at first, fifteen were purchased to serve their redemption time working for Sir George Yardley the Governor of Virginia. He was the proprietor of the thousand acre Flowerdew Hundred Plantation. By the 1630's, the colony through the use of the Africans, had established a successful economy based on tobacco.

Slavery was born and soon after, slave trading became big business. These human souls were acquired in Africa for an average price of about twenty-five dollars each - paid primarily in merchandise. They were sold in the Americas for about one hundred fifty dollars. As the price of slaves increased, so did the inhumane overcrowding of the ships. This was the beginning of the worst crime ever inflicted upon a people and the most morally reprehensible agenda the world has ever known. Adding to this injustice, and more horrifying, was that the perpetrators claimed a religious manifestation that justified the crime.

From this fateful day, and for the next two-hundred years, people of African descent suffered a perpetual holocaust in this country. It was done through a designed, systematic effort to destroy millions of lives through indoctrination, brutality, savagery, and terror. I am always struck by the use of the word civilization in this matter because the root word is "civil" and there was nothing civil about the institution of slavery. To be clear, a slave is chattel – a human being considered property and servant for life. The business of slave trading had one purpose – profit.

Now, if capturing and stealing the victims was not misery enough what was to follow surely was in every sense of the word. The devastating effects of bondage would have lifelong mental consequences on a race of people for centuries to come. The people involved in this terror proclaimed that a slave was born. I strongly disagree with that premise. A slave was made by means of a defined calculated plan structured for the purpose of being a beast of burden. We know the reasons for this atrocity – to build a nation and for the benefit of profit. But what is not understood, is how it was designed to be sustainable. That part has become little more than a footnote to history.

I am reminded of the powerful words once spoken by the great heroin Harriet Tubman who expressed succinctly the effectiveness of this wretched system of mental conditioning. She was asked shortly before her death, if she knew how many slaves she freed while conducting the Underground Railroad. She did not think about it replying quickly, *"I could have freed a lot more, if they had only known they were slaves."*

From that day in 1619, when the first Africans were dragged onto the shores of Jamestown to the present where we've witnessed the first African American to be elected President of these United States (or as Jesse would put it – *from the outhouse to the White House*) - there is no doubt our story is the greatest story ever told. Maybe a passage from scripture would be more fitting -*"the first shall be last and the last shall be first."* Nonetheless, there was a plan, a sinister master plan, conceived at some point to ensure that people of our hue remained *"the least of thee"*.

As the story goes, a British slave owner from the West Indies was invited to the colony of Virginia sometime during the year 1712 to teach his methods to slave owners. Willie Lynch was the name of this man credited with a speech delivered on the banks of the James River. It is noteworthy to mention that the James River was named for the diabolical King of England who, by the way, is the same guy responsible for the twenty-eighth version of the esteemed Holy Bible.

Lynch brought with him, as he put it, a foolproof method for controlling black slaves that will last for three hundred years maybe even a thousand years. Consequently, as of this writing, his prophetic prophesy will hit its mark in 2012. It is believed the term "lynching" was derived from his last name as a way to pay homage to this man for delivering this ingenious approach. The name Willie Lynch is interesting because it may be a simple play on words. For example, Will Lynch or Will he Lynch. Whatever the reason, it no doubt had significant psychological implications that played heavily on a naive race of people.

> Lynch began this historic presentation with a warm greeting: *"Gentlemen, you know what your problems are; I do not need to elaborate. I am not here to enumerate your problems. I am here to introduce you to a method of solving them. In my bag here, I have a foolproof method for controlling your black slaves. I guarantee every one of you that if installed correctly it will control the slaves for at least three hundred years. My method is simple...The black slave after receiving this indoctrination shall carry on and will become self-refueling and self-generating for hundreds of years, maybe thousands...."* The seeds of devastation were fertilized and the process of destruction was underway for the making of an entire race into slaves.

In the speech, Lynch outlined a number of differences among the slaves. He stressed to his audience that they should take these differences and make them bigger. These differences included such things as age, color, intelligence, fine hair vs. coarse hair, tall vs. short, male vs. female. These tactics were not new. However they were more than likely put together collectively for this specific purpose for the first time as keys to control.

This short eight paragraph speech was profound in that it was the embodiment of the cruelest demoralizing agenda ever imposed upon a people since the days when the Romans crucified our Lord. As Lynch closed his speech that day, he said, *"They must love, respect, and trust only us."* This is the key to producing a successful strategy. Whether this story is true or not is cause for much speculation. However, as history demonstrates a manufactured plan was developed by someone to achieve these results that continue to this day.

The supposed Willie Lynch letter first appeared in the early 1970's gaining widespread attention during the nineties when it began appearing on the Internet. Since then it has often been promoted as an authentic account of slavery during the 18th century but its inaccuracies and anachronisms have led historians to conclude that it is a hoax. I don't think any reasonable person would believe those persons present, if there was a meeting, took written notes.

However, the same reasonable thinking person can see that there was a designed plan created by someone in order to sustain such a system to derive huge economic returns. It may have been something as simple as "divide and conquer" that has been used so successfully over time. Even if we assume the Willie Lynch story a modern creation. In principle, the concept was ingenious and more than the biggest urban myth ever.

So you see Boo, this then begs the question, why are we still fighting amongst ourselves. Furthermore, how can the ruling people, or anyone for that matter, justify a philosophy for building and maintaining a government which sanctioned murder, among other atrocities, to enslave human beings? I know what I am telling you will never be taught in a classroom. I know because I was not taught this in school nor did anyone explain that our government, through legislative sessions, passed laws to ensure that our bondage was sustained.

You must know that this brutally wicked system was sanctioned by the church in the name of God. Therefore, it is important to recognize that when the church endorsed slavery and the vehicle that drove it. This meant in the eyes of the system - God himself authorized this immoral agenda. If this was the mentality of the church, which is a historical fact that religion sanctioned and justified enslaving people for centuries. I have to wonder does this way of thinking still exist.

So I say to you that tomorrow ended yesterday and this minute starts today, and that is called your future. Therefore, we need to search our souls for truth to secure understanding to be made whole. Boo, it is from the bottom of my heart and a continued prayer that we will be able to one day, as a people, all people, join hands and sing that old Negro spiritual, "Free at last, free at last. Thank God Almighty, we are free at last."

Chapter Twelve

This bright eyed little boy seemed immersed in every word I was saying and for that I was pleased. I am certain he had never been taken on such a historical journey. Couple it with the monumental event of this day - WOW! I can only describe it as something of biblical proportions. When you consider America's racial past, the election of a black man to be president made it very special. Unfortunately, the youth of today have no concept of the brutality and bigotry of America's hidden history. Naturally, my grandson wanted to know more.

I used the word history not realizing that I misspoke. My attentive grandson quickly corrected me "you mean His-Story don't you granddad." With a big smile I looked at my grandson knowing that he was absorbing the knowledge of this oral history being shared. I agreed that I did err and continued telling him that there have been many methods used to suppress people over time. Unfortunately, African Americans have had to endure the brunt of these deviant behaviors.

I can tell you that the history of America reports that African Americans were not the only ones subjected to these indignities. What I can report is that it has always been minority groups. It's just been African Americans who've been so brutally affected by laws designed to ensure that our people remained a permanent underclass. All other groups, with the exception of the American Indian, moved out of that station.

It is a fact, from slavery to modern time's explicit laws, from the Constitution to State laws and codes were specifically designed and implemented to ensure that this system of bondage enslaved people of African descent. This is particularly significant with respect to the election of Mr. Obama because our station was created and enforced by legislation, making African Americans second-class citizens or as the Constitution says, in effect, less than human.

Supreme Court cases like the *Dread Scott Decision* or *Plessey v Ferguson* remind us that African Americans were on the short end of the long arm of the law. This ideology began with indentured servants, then slavery, segregation, Jim Crow and now – could it be conservatism? During each period of racial classification the laws which were enacted and imposed upon people of color were called - Black Codes. I suppose it makes these immoral sanctions sound kinder.

Black Codes were laws designed and passed specifically to take civil rights and liberties away from African Americans usually, on state and local levels. I would argue that this is the reason today's conservatives dream of "states' rights" and speak of taking back their country. Because, at the state level they can be unimpeded in turning back the hands of time. Most of the discriminatory legislation in terms of Black Codes was used most often by southern states to control labor, movements and activities of the newly freed slaves at the end of the Civil War.

When I say southern states I am reminded of how Malcolm X put it, "anywhere south of Canada is south," meaning wherever you were in America you were subjected to discrimination by the *"separate but equal"* laws of the land. Boo, you need to know that the Black Codes of the 1860's were not the same as the Jim Crow laws. The Black Codes were a reaction to the eradication of slavery and the South's defeat in the Civil War. Southern legislatures enacted them during Reconstruction and the Jim Crow era nearer to the end of the 19th century after Reconstruction. Although unwritten, Jim Crow was the law of the land.

Then, there were sundown laws that meant black people could not live or be caught in certain towns after dark. In some cases, signs were placed at the town's borders with statements similar to the one posted in Hawthorne California in the 1930's that read, "Nigger, Don't Let The Sun Set On YOU In Hawthorne." Imagine that! In some cases, exclusions were official town policy enforced through restrictive covenants or the policy was enforced through intimidation.

Let me be clear, a sundown town was a town that was all white on purpose. They were also sometimes known as "sunset towns" or "gray towns." The term was widely used in the United States in areas from Ohio to Oregon but they were most prevalent in the south. Even in Canada, many towns in Southern Ontario, Alberta and Quebec were sundown towns prior to 1982 when they were outlawed.

Before slavery was abolished by the Thirteenth Amendment of the United States Constitution, African Americans were considered three-fifths human. Therefore, all former slave states adopted Black Codes. During 1865 every southern state passed such Codes restricting freedmen and former slaves who were emancipated but not full citizens. While the southern states pursued re-admission into the Union these efforts were designed to ensure that the freedmen had limited second class civil rights and no voting rights. Freedmen were black people who were granted their freedom after the Civil War when slavery was supposed to have ended.

After winning large majorities in the 1866 elections the Republicans put the south under military rule. They held new elections in which the freedmen could vote. The new governments repealed all the Black Codes. They were never reenacted - officially anyway. The Black Codes that were enacted immediately after the Civil War, though varying from state to state, were all intended to secure a steady supply of cheap labor in order to continue the inferiority of the freed slaves. Black Codes had their roots in the slave codes that had formerly been in effect.

Having convinced themselves that slavery was justified, many planters feared African Americans wouldn't work without coercion. The Black Codes were an attempt to control them and to ensure they did not claim social equality. These Black Codes outraged public opinion in the north because it seemed as if the south was creating a form of quasi-slavery to evade the results of the war.

These injustices have been erased from history, which is why it's my job to teach you what others will not. As I talked, I could see dismay written on my grandson's face but I continued the "learning".

The premise behind chattel slavery in America was that slaves were property and, as such, they had no legal rights. The slave codes in their many forms were seen as effective tools against slave unrest, particularly as a hedge against uprisings and runaways. Enforcement of slave codes also varied but corporal punishment was widely and harshly employed. The "Runaway Slave Laws" made it mandatory by law that all whites do their duty to return, turn in or capture any slave suspected of being a runaway. There were also bounties and rewards provided for such "patriotism".

For example, the Eleventh Legislature of Texas produced these codes in 1866. The intent of the legislation was to reaffirm the inferior position held by slaves and free blacks in antebellum Texas and to regulate black labor. The codes reflected the unwillingness of white Texans to accept blacks as equals. Thus, the codes continued legal discrimination between whites and blacks.

Boo, this is a very important; His-Story tells us that during the Civil War Abraham Lincoln freed the slaves with a stroke of his pen. Unfortunately, like most of what His-Story tells us, this is not exactly true and this misconception has been embedded into the consciousness of our minds. What is true; Abraham Lincoln did issue the Emancipation Proclamation on September 22, 1862 with an effective date of January 1, 1863. The proclamation abolished slavery in the Confederate States of America. The reality is that it had minimal immediate effect on most slaves' day-to-day lives, neither in the south nor in the union states. Texas was particularly resistant as the state refused to recognize Lincoln's proclamation order.

Have you ever heard of Juneteenth? Well, let me tell you why Juneteenth became infamous. It became necessary for the Union to send 2,000 federal troops to Galveston, Texas under the command of General Gordon Granger to take possession of the state. Their mission was to bring the word of freedom to the quarter-million slaves residing in the state and enforce the emancipation of its slaves. It's likely that none of them had any idea that they had actually been freed more than two years earlier; a day of mass emancipation.

Legend has it that on June 19, 1865, while standing on the balcony of Galveston's Ashton Villa Granger read the contents of "General Order No. 3" that said:

The people of Texas are informed that, in accordance with a proclamation from the Executive of the United States, all slaves are free. This involves an absolute equality of personal rights and rights of property between former masters and slaves, and the connection heretofore existing between them becomes that between employer and hired labor. The freedmen are advised to remain quietly at their present homes and work for wages. They are informed that they will not be allowed to collect at military posts and that they will not be supported in idleness either there or elsewhere.

June 19th has since become known as Juneteenth, a name derived from a combination of the words June and nineteenth. Juneteenth celebrations began in Texas the following year with former slaves in Galveston rejoicing in the streets with jubilant celebrations. Across many parts of Texas, freed individuals pooled their funds to purchase land specifically for their communities' increasingly large Juneteenth gatherings. In many communities to this very day, Juneteenth celebrations include a wide range of festivities, such as parades, street fairs, cookouts, park parties with music, dancing, and contests of physical strength and intellect.

This celebration for many African Americans is a de facto Independence Day commemorating the end of slavery. There are many in the African America community who advocate Juneteenth as deserving the same recognition as Independence Day. When you think about the American struggle; we may have gotten here in different ways and at different times but many African Americans feel you can't really celebrate freedom in America by just acknowledging the Fourth of July, especially since freedom was not granted to African Americans at that time.

Only the state of Texas celebrates it as a legal state holiday. The tradition spread to bordering Southern states, such as Arkansas and Louisiana, as migrating African Americans fanned out from Texas. Currently, a little more than half of U.S. states acknowledge Juneteenth in some form or another usually, on the third Saturday of June. Twelve other states list it as an official holiday, including Arkansas, New York, Massachusetts, Connecticut, and Alaska. The annual observance is held in 26 of the 50 states and its unofficial observance also takes place in several countries.

San Francisco, California has held one of the nation's largest Juneteenth celebrations for the last five-plus decades with Minneapolis boasting the largest festival. Yet as one would expect from an unofficial holiday its popularity has waned over the decades. It fell from favor during the civil rights struggles of the 1950's and 60's as African Americans looked more to change their future rather than focus on their past.

Following a resurgence of popularity in the 70's, Texas state legislator Al Edwards introduced a bill in 1979 to make Juneteenth a state holiday, with the first state-approved celebration taking place the following year. Edwards is sometimes referred to as the father of Juneteenth and one of many who have been working to make it a national holiday. In years past, Senator Barack Obama, now the president-elect, co-sponsored legislation to make Juneteenth a national holiday.

It's a bittersweet holiday; a time for celebration, reflection, healing and, hopefully, a time for the country to come together and acknowledge its legacy. Today, Juneteenth recognizes African American freedom and emphasizes education and achievement. It is a time marked for remembrance of all that has happened in this country. In the end, our survival depends upon the willingness of all races to unite and live as one people. Juneteenth brings us one step closer to that dream.

Now, back to Texas - the legislature amended the 1856 penal code. It emphasized the continuing line between whites and blacks by defining all individuals with one-eighth or more African blood as persons of color subject to special provisions in the law. Minorities were systematically excluded from living in or, sometimes even passing through, a sundown town after sunset. This allowed maids and workmen to provide unskilled labor during the day. Sociologists have described this as the nadir of American race relations.

Sundown towns existed throughout the nation. You may be surprised to learn that many were located in northern states that were not pre-Civil

War slave states. There have not been any de jure sundown towns in the country since legislation was passed in the 1960's inspired by the Civil Rights Movement. With that said, de facto sundown towns and counties where no black families could live still exist. Today, for example, if you were to go to a million dollar gated community, you might see such a place. We see hints of it in class structure or economic racism that has risen to the surface of society's consciousness, particularly in this political climate.

The Civil Rights Movement of the 1950's and 1960's and especially the Civil Rights Act of 1968 prohibited racial discrimination in the sale, rental, and financing of housing. That caused the number of sundown towns to decrease. However, as sociologists suggest it is impossible to precisely count the number of sundown towns at any given time because most towns did not keep records of the ordinances or signs that marked their sundown status.

It is important for you to understand - sundown status meant African Americans or non-whites who came into town after sundown were subject to harassment, threats, and violent acts – up to and including lynching. This was necessary, at least in the minds of the bigots, because slavery fixed the status of most blacks, so there was no need for statutory measures segregating the races therefore "racial segregation was hardly a new phenomenon." These restrictive Black Codes morphed in one form or another to achieve the desired effects of maintaining superior status for whites.

Boo, this careful review of our history is imperative in that understanding the past will greatly benefit you in life. You must know history as truth, for it will open your mind to what the future may present. It was King Solomon who said, "There is nothing new under the sun". In other words, history has a way of repeating itself. Therefore, if you don't know where you came from you will never get to where you are going.

Chapter Thirteen

I must admit, I love this stuff. I mean "History". Moreover, debunking the myths and misrepresentations of "His Story" by using truth to empower my grandson was wholesomely empowering for me. Thankfully, Boo was captivated almost to the point of being consumed. While I continued to examine that which is our past, I thought I would ask my grandson if he knew "Jim Crow". His response was, "does he Rap?" Surprised by that response I wondered if society had conditioned, no - crippled our children's minds to the point of believing this is all black people are appreciated for. I suppose as much as I hate to admit it, this unfortunately seems to be the case.

As I continued, I told him that Jim Crow was a real person and his name came to be identified with the awful era of segregation. Today's youth have no idea nor can they relate to the dehumanizing indignities and degradation that were imposed upon our forefathers by segregation.

I want you to know the origin of certain terms that were used to identify indignities like the term Jim Crow. It originated in a song performed by Daddy Rice a white minstrel show entertainer in the 1830's. Rice, a white man, covered his face with charcoal paste or burnt cork to resemble a black man. He sang and danced a routine in the caricature of a silly black person. By the 1850's this belittling blackface character, one of several stereotypical images of black inferiority in American popular culture, was a standard act in minstrel shows of the day.

The term Jim Crow became synonymous with the concept of segregation directed specifically at African Americans in the late nineteenth-century. It is not clear why this term was selected. However, what is clear is that by 1900, the term was generally used to identify with those racist laws and actions that deprived African Americans of their civil rights by presenting them as inferiors and subordinates.

This term entered into the lexicon of racial bigotry after the landmark U.S. Supreme Court decision of *Plessey vs. Ferguson* in 1896. The case was brought by the New Orleans Committee of Citizens who arranged for Homer Plessey's arrest in order to challenge Louisiana's separate-but-equal segregation laws. Subsequently, Jim Crow appeared in many southern states as they tried to thwart the gains made during Reconstruction following the Civil War.

The argument was "we, as freemen, still believe that we were right and our cause is sacred" referring to the new south. The Supreme Court disagreed and as a result of that fateful decision, a policy of segregation became the law of the land that lasted for more than sixty years. Reconstruction allowed African Americans to make great progress in building their own institutions, passing civil rights laws, and electing officials to public office. In response to these achievements southern whites launched a vicious illegal war against southern blacks and their white allies.

In most places whites carried out this war under the cover of secret organizations such as the KKK. Thousands of African Americans were terrorized in those bloody years. The federal government attempted to stop the bloodshed by sending in troops and holding investigations, but its efforts were far too limited and frankly were not intended to solve the problem. Remember that anywhere south of Canada was south.

Black resistance to segregation was difficult because the system of land tenancy, known as sharecropping, left most blacks economically dependent upon landlords and merchant suppliers. In addition, white terror at the hands of lynch mobs threatened all members of the black family. This reality made it nearly impossible for blacks to stand up to Jim Crow because such actions might bring the wrath of the white mob on one's parents, brothers, spouse and children.

Frankly, few black families were economically well off enough to buck the local white power structure of banks, merchants, and landlords. To put it succinctly: impoverished and often illiterate southern blacks were in a weak position to confront the racist culture of Jim Crow. To enforce the new legal order of segregation southern whites often resorted to even more brutalizing acts of mob terror including race riots. Ritualized lynchings were regularly practiced to enforce this immoral agenda.

Some historians see this extremely brutal and endemic commitment of white supremacy as breaking with the South's more laissez-faire and paternalistic past. Others view this "new order" as a more rigid continuation of the "cult of whiteness" at work in the south to maintain power. Both perspectives agree that the 1890's ushered in a more formal racist south. One in which white supremacists used the law and mob terror to restrict the lives of African Americans and popularize a culture in which African American people were considered inferior.

Chapter Fourteen

We finished breakfast and I suggested it was time to start the day. My plan was to ride the go-cart for a while. I was thinking something like this would be exciting but Boo had another idea. He wanted to go fishing. This came as a total surprise because what little boy does not have gas on his chest. Not to mention, it was early November and a bit chilly. So I asked, "Why do you want to go fishing?" He responded, "You told me that story about my dad and it's a way to be close to him Granddad". I was touched and like any grandfather, in spite of the chill in the air, I said, "OK".

The story my grandson referred to was my admission that I had never taken his dad fishing. It is one of my biggest regrets. My son, Jarad, would ask me to take him fishing as he was growing up but because of my job, ambition, and other things; I viewed it as unimportant at the time. I wrongly assumed that we would have plenty of time to enjoy fishing along with all of the other joys of life. So, posthumously, this was a special treat for the two of us. It was a way for us to feel close to my son.

As we arrived at the pier on the beach that we frequented; I was not all that surprised to find few people strolling along the water's edge in spite of the air being a bit chilly, but comfortable. We brought a couple of folding chairs and some snacks as we found our way to the spot where we'd hoped the fish would be biting. Though cool, it was a beautiful day with just enough of a breeze to create very small white-caps on the water's surface. It was also clear enough that we could see across the bay to the Eastern Shore. The beach is on the Chesapeake Bay which is about seven miles wide. On a clear day the other shore can be seen, which incidentally is where Boo lives.

Once our lines where cast I said, "I've told you a lot about our historic past. I've told you about segregation and Jim Crow becoming the law of the land. I've talked to you about how the rule of "separate but equal" had dreadful consequences. Now, let me tell you a true story about one of America's most reprehensible secrets – a secret that has been hidden from view for nearly a century." We relaxed on the pier watching the waves wash upon the shore and I began the next lesson.

Boo, during the Jim Crow era, black people were segregated in all areas of life and faced odds that were against all odds. We were relegated, by law, to live in communities almost completely separate from White America. With that said, I want you to know the richness and great history of these communities that I like to call "Brownsville". Almost every American town had such a place because of America's de facto system of apartheid. People of African descent were forced to live in communities and depend on one another in order to survive, and survive they did.

The most infamous segregated community of them all was in Tulsa, Oklahoma. Most people are not aware that the State of Oklahoma was set aside to be a Black and Indian state. It is worth noting that nearly a third of the people who traveled the terrifying "Trail of Tears" alongside the Indians from 1830 to 1842 - were black people.

Although it was in an unusual location, this "Brownsville" came to be known as "Black Wall Street". It served as a prime example of the typical black community of the era that did business far beyond anyone's expectations. Actually, this story is about the rise and fall of this magnificent community. I'm not sure what he expected me to say next, but he was listening and holding on to every word in anticipation.

The name, "Black Wall Street", was fittingly given to this community because it was the most affluent all-black community in America. It was known as the golden door of the black community during the early 1900's. It was the epitome of success and proved that African Americans could build a solid infrastructure and secure a profitable future themselves.

At that time, Oklahoma included over 28 black townships. The citizens of Oklahoma chose a black governor; there were PhD's, black attorneys, doctors and professionals from all walks of life contributing to the successful development of this community. One such luminous figure was Dr. Berry who also owned the bus system which generated an average income of $500 a day in 1910. In addition, during this time physicians owned medical schools to empower and develop African Americans.

Black Wall Street encompassed 36 square blocks with over 600 businesses. It had a population of 15,000 African Americans. There were pawn shops, brothels, jewelry stores, churches, restaurants and movie theaters. Their success was monumentally evident in that the entire State of Oklahoma had only two airports; yet six blacks owned their own planes. Just to show how wealthy many black people were, there was a banker in a neighboring town whose wife, California Taylor, would take a cruise to Paris every three months to shop and have her clothes made. Her father owned the largest cotton gin west of the Mississippi.

There was also a man named Mason in nearby Wagner County who had the largest potato farm in the west. When he harvested, he would fill one hundred boxcars a day. Another black man not far away was doing the same thing with a spinach farm. The typical family averaged five children or more though the typical farm family would have ten or more children who made up the nucleus of the labor.

What was significant about Black Wall Street was that people understood a very important principle – they kept their money in their communities. The dollars circulated 36 to 1,000 times within the community; sometimes taking a year for currency to leave the community. This is something the African American community of today does not fully appreciate or practice. Today, a dollar will leave the black community within fifteen minutes. The Black Wall Street community was so tight and wealthy simply because they traded dollars hand-to-hand. Nepotism contributed greatly to the success of this community as a way to help one another – a tactic that needs to be instilled in our culture today. Furthermore, it was because of the harsh Jim Crow laws that they had to depend upon one another.

This community also understood the significance of education. One of their founding principles was to ensure the education for every child. They understood that education was knowledge and knowledge was power. Suits and ties were worn in school. Moreover, morals and respect were taught at a young age.

An unprecedented amount of global business was conducted from within the Black Wall Street community, which flourished from the early 1900's until 1921. Then, the unthinkable happened. The community faced its valley or more accurately stated; it was destroyed. This community suffered the largest massacre of non-military Americans in the history of this country - a massacre which has been hidden from view for over a hundred years.

As you might imagine, low-income whites looked over and saw how prosperous the black community had become and they destroyed it. I don't know the true reason – jealousy was mentioned, but racism was certainly at its core. The Tulsa Race Riot led by the infamous Ku Klux Klan working in concert with ranking city officials and other sympathizers was lethal.

On Tuesday evening, June 1, 1921, the most affluent all-black community in America was bombed from the air and burned to the ground by mobs of resentful whites. In a period spanning fewer than twelve hours, the once thriving black business district in northern Tulsa lay smoldering. This model community was destroyed and a major African American economic movement was resoundingly defused.

The result of this rampage left some 3,000 African Americans dead and over 600 successful businesses lost. Among them were 21 churches, 21 restaurants, 30 grocery stores and two movie theaters, plus a hospital, a bank, a post office, libraries, schools, law offices, a half-dozen private airplanes and even the bus system. You would think this historic event would be common knowledge - but not so. There is no mention of it in "His-Story".

One is hard-pressed to find any documentation concerning the incident let alone an accurate accounting of it. Not in any reference or American history books will you find a record of one of the worst incidents of violence ever visited upon people of African descent. This night of horror was unimaginable. Try to imagine seeing 1,500 homes being burned and looted while white families with their children stood around the borders of the community watching the massacre much in the same manner as they would watch a lynching. It must have been beyond belief for the victims.

This atrocity occurred as a result of black prosperity. A lot of white folks had come back from World War I and they were dirt poor. They looked over into this thriving black community and saw black men who had returned from the war as heroes and they resented it. It cost this community everything. Justice and reconciliation are often unreachable goals as history proves. So, as you can imagine son, not a single dime of restitution was ever provided; no insurance claim was awarded to a single victim.

I know you are not aware of this little known history fact or some say urban myth. Let me tell you where the word "picnic" came from. It is believed, at least in our community, that it was typical to have a picnic on a Friday evening in Oklahoma. The word was short for "pick a nigger" to lynch. They would lynch a black male for entertainment and usually cut off body parts to keep as souvenirs. This went on every weekend in many parts of the country with thousands lynched in the first half of the last century. There were thousands of black victims killed - usually black men. As despicable as that is, true or not, this is my understanding as to the true origin of the word. It is a shame because in our consciousness today we participate in outdoor gatherings as a celebration with most not realizing the roots of what we call a picnic.

There is also another code-word coming out of Oklahoma that you should know. It is how the term "Sooner" came into the lexicon of the American conscience. This term was used as the earliest form of Affirmative Action for white settlers who reached the territories in the west. It meant the sooner you got there, the sooner you could claim the land, which actually belonged to the Indians. So, it is important to remember that words have meaning. The meaning comes from somewhere and is often subversive.

To restate my point there are milestones, mountains, and valleys in every life; surely this community of proud people experienced them all. It is imperative that you learn these lessons because those who ignore the lessons of the past are doomed to see them repeated. Just remember life is not a race you run. It is a relay and I believe it is my responsibility to pass the baton. The youth of today must be able to look at our communities with the knowledge that we are the descendants of kings.

As you can see murder was a powerful weapon in the arsenal of those who exercised racial terror campaigns for the purpose of intimidating and controlling blacks during slavery, segregation, and beyond. Let me give you another example of this horrendous truth. On August 24, 1955, a fourteen year-old child whose name was Emmett Till, a resident of Chicago, supposedly whistled at a white woman in a grocery store in the southern town of Money, Mississippi.

Till, just a child and from the north, didn't understand that he had broken an unwritten Jim Crow law. Three days later two white men dragged him from his bed in the dead of night, beat him brutally, then shot him in the head. As if this was not horrible enough, his killers were arrested, charged with murder and both were acquitted in a matter of hours by an all-white, all-male jury. Shortly after the acquittal, the defendants sold their story to a journalist including a detailed account of how they murdered this young child.

The murder and the trial horrified the nation. Till's death was a spark that helped ignite the Civil Rights Movement. Three months after his body was pulled from the Tallahatchie River, the Montgomery bus boycott began. The boycott not only was the beginning of the end of segregation laws, it was responsible for introducing the world to Rev. Martin Luther King, Jr.

It's just been a few generations since that fateful night. I still struggle to find the words to describe this heinous crime which has yet to receive justice. So I'll share with you the powerful words of Maya Angelou: "History, despite its wrenching pain, cannot be unlived, but if faced with courage, need not be lived again."

Chapter Fifteen

If you can imagine watching the reels of a movie, like Roots for example, my resurrecting this history in the oral tradition of our ancestors proved to be the perfect bond for my grandson and me. I know telling him about "Black Wall Street" the most prosperous segregated community and the horrible stain left upon America's past, albeit hidden, was unbelievable and painful.

At this point, I thought this was a good time to tell my grandson about the most famous Brownsville community of them all. Surely it would be positive and uplifting for his young mind. Boo the place I want to tell you about I like to refer to as the Black Mecca and once known as the "Capital of Black America." The place that held this honored destination goes to Harlem USA. There is no other place on earth with such a profound storied tradition.

Harlem, always a cultural icon, began as a European settlement established in July 1639 and was known then as New Harlem. The English took control of the colony in 1658, changing the hamlet's name to Harlem. At that time, it was merely a small agricultural town just outside of New York City. The name Harlem was a synonym for elegant living through a good part of the nineteenth century. It was also home to the estate of Alexander Hamilton.

In 1893, the Harlem Monthly Magazine wrote: "it is evident to the most superficial observer that the center of fashion, wealth, culture and intelligence, must, in the near future, be found in the ancient and honorable village of Harlem." Even then Harlem seemed ordained to be the center of cultural significance but it was not until the mass migration of blacks in 1904 that it began to flourish as a predominantly black enclave.

Harlem became prominent to the African American community as a result of a real estate crash that worsened conditions for blacks throughout New York City. This prompted Philip Payton, owner of the Afro American

Realty Company, to almost single-handedly create the migration of blacks from their previous neighborhoods. This ultimately established Black Harlem or "Uptown" as it came to be known.

Shortly thereafter, Black churches began to move uptown and the transformation was complete. St. Philip's Episcopal Church purchased an entire block of buildings on West 135th Street to rent to members of its congregation. Black Harlem with its extensive real estate holdings has always been a religious community with over 400 churches of every faith. These churches were to become very influential because of their large congregations and wealth. They operated in storefronts, basements and converted townhouses; just as many do today.

At the same time blacks migrated to northern industrial cities fueled by their desire to leave behind the Jim Crow south and seek better jobs and education for their children. Jobs were abundant and many blacks were able to obtain work as a result of the industries needing black laborers to fill new jobs in support of the war effort. They migrated north, in most cases, to escape a culture of lynching and violence in the brutal southern states.

By 1920, a mere twenty years later, Harlem became the center of a flowering black culture that became known as the Harlem Renaissance. This period witnessed the greatest collection of artistic production creating the sounds and entertainment of the Roaring Twenties. Its influence changed America. Ironically, blacks were sometimes excluded from viewing what their peers were creating because of segregation. Some of the jazz venues, most notably the famed Cotton Club where Duke Ellington played and Connie's Inn, were restricted to whites only, although some uptown clubs were integrated.

The most famous venue in Harlem was the world renowned Apollo Theater that opened on January 26, 1934 on 125th Street in what had been a burlesque house. It is best known for its "Amateur Night at the Apollo" that continues to this very day. The Apollo was a proving ground of sorts for black entertainers; "if you could make it there you could make it anywhere". Every black performer was ordained by its audience in one way or another. I don't have enough time to tell you the names of all of the greats that graced the Apollo stage. I can tell you if they wanted to be successful, they played the Apollo Theater.

Another famous spot uptown was the Savoy Ballroom on Lenox Avenue known for swing dancing. It was immortalized in a popular song of the era - "Stompin' at the Savoy." During the 1920's and 1930's, between Lenox and Seventh Avenues, central Harlem had over 125 entertainment places operating including speakeasies, cellars, lounges, cafes, taverns, supper clubs, rib joints, theaters, dance halls, bars and grills. The place was jumpin!

Harlem served as the home and key inspiration to generations of novelists, poets, musicians, and actors throughout the twentieth century; particularly during the Harlem Renaissance. Because of the city's pace, the diversity of its backgrounds, the difficulties and experiences associated with living in Harlem, the hamlet was full of great talent that found expression in theater, fiction, and music, among other art forms.

Some of the luminaries Harlem produced were Paul Robeson, Claude McKay, and Langston Hughes just to name a few. In addition to its storied musicians and writers, the community also hosted countless actors and theater companies. They included the likes of the New Heritage Repertory Theater, National Black Theater, Lafayette Players, Harlem Suitcase Theater, the Negro Playwrights, American Negro Theater, and the Rose McClendon Players. Arthur Mitchell, a former dancer with the New York City Ballet, established the Dance Theatre of Harlem as a school for classical ballet and theater training in the late 1960's.

Harlem is also home to notable contemporary artists such as the Harlem Boys' Choir. This famous touring choir serves as an education program for young men, most of whom are black. There is also a Girls' Choir of Harlem and both companies have toured the world. Harlem is also credited with the creation of hip-hop and many hip-hop dances associated with this genre. It is known for producing rappers Kurtis Blow and hip-hop Mogul P. Diddy or Puff Daddy.

After the romantic era of the Harlem Renaissance this renowned community ceased to be home to a majority of New York City's blacks. The character of the community changed in the years after the World War II as middle-class blacks left for the outer boroughs and suburbs. With the increase of a poorer population the neighborhood began to deteriorate and some of the storied traditions of the Harlem Renaissance gave way to poverty, crime or other social ills.

I explained to my grandson that the character of a community is determined by its members and the rich history of Harlem could not be told in a few words. I don't think anyone can capture the essence of Harlem's greatness without talking about "The Underworld." Aside from the countless artistic achievements; what was most romanticized was the role the underworld played in the nightlife and social scene.

During the 1920's, the Jewish and Italian mafia played major roles in running the whites-only nightclubs and the speakeasies that catered to white audiences. Famous mobsters, such as Dutch Schultz, controlled all liquor production and distribution in Harlem during prohibition. Rather than compete with the established mobs, black gangsters concentrated on the "policy racket" also called the "numbers game." This was a gambling scheme similar to today's lottery that could be played, illegally, from countless locations around Harlem.

By the early 1950's, the total money at play amounted to billions of dollars and the police force had been thoroughly corrupted by bribes from the numbers bosses. When you talk about Harlem gangsters, particularly of that era, two names immediately come to mind. One of the most powerful early numbers bosses was a woman, Madame Stephanie St. Clair, a black French woman from Martinique known as Madame Queen. It is said that she was a tall abrasive tough woman with a seldom-seen gentle side. She was ruthless enough to be the leader of the infamous Forty Thieves, a New York extortion gang.

The Forty Thieves had such a notorious reputation for being tough that even the white gangsters would not interfere with their illegal operations or attempt to take over their turf. Madame Queen utilized her experience and talents to set up operations as a policy banker and recruited some of Harlem's most noteworthy gangsters in support of her growing numbers business. Within a year, she was worth more than $500,000 with more than forty runners and ten comptrollers in her charge.

The other notorious gangster of the day was the legendary Ellsworth "Bumpy" Johnson known as the Godfather of Harlem. You may recall Lawrence Fishburn played Bumpy Johnson in the movie "Hoodlum." Bumpy was one of Madame Queen's main recruits. He was a colorful character from Charleston, South Carolina, who moved to Harlem with his parents when he was a small boy. He was given the nickname Bumpy because of a large bump on the back of his head.

He was a dapper gangster who always made a point to wear the latest and most stylish clothes while flashing wads of cash wherever he went. Bumpy was a pimp, burglar and stickup man who possessed a headstrong attitude. He always carried a knife and gun, which he would not hesitate to use. Bumpy feared nobody and did not shy away from confrontation. He was known for having a short fuse and his famed arrogance served to instigate several barroom clashes over the slightest issue.

He never learned to curb his temper or to bow his head to any man. His combative nature caused him to spend nearly half his life in prisons before he reached the age of 30. Bumpy also proved to be an incorrigible prisoner, spending one-third of a ten-year sentence in solitary confinement. During his incarcerations, he became an avid reader and began writing poetry. But, because of his attitude, he was shuttled from prison to prison until his release in 1932.

Despite his tough-guy reputation Bumpy had a soft side. It was common knowledge among Harlemites that he often helped many of Harlem's poor with secret cash donations and gifts. Madame Queen liked what she saw in Bumpy and offered him a position as henchman in her numbers racket. He accepted and quickly gained her trust. One of his first tasks was to confront the Bub Hewlett gang, which was one of Harlem's most notorious gangs that wanted to control the entire numbers game in Harlem. It erupted into one of Harlem's most violent and bloody gang wars. Eventually, Bumpy defeated Hewlett temporarily saving the numbers game from the Mob's first takeover attempt.

The relationship between these two towering figures was strange and tenuous at best. Some said they had an ongoing affair. Although most people of the day said, albeit an odd couple, they were only business partners. Bumpy never abandoned his pimping and robbery professions, both of which irritated Madame Queen. Together, however, they knew how to make the numbers game a success and peacefully coexisted. These bosses became financial powerhouses providing capital for loans for those who could not qualify for them from traditional financial institutions, in other words, loan sharking. They invested in legitimate businesses and real estate as a way to legitimize their profits.

The Godfather of Harlem lived until 1968 dying of a heart attack as opposed to dying by the gun in the manner so many did in his business. As a testament to his success he maintained control of the underworld for nearly forty years. Some said nothing illegal took place in Harlem without his permission. After Bumpy's death the underworld became loosely organized and overcome by the drug trade with its many factions. In that environment, Bumpy's protégé Frank Lucas and his rival Nicky Barnes became the most dominant players in the game.

Frank Lucas operated the largest drug business in Harlem during the late 1960's and early 1970's. He was particularly known for cutting out the middle man in the drug trade and buying heroin directly from sources in the Golden Triangle of Thailand. Lucas boasted that he smuggled heroin in the coffins of dead American servicemen. He controlled such large quantities of heroin that he even supplied the Mafia.

Lucas was notorious and powerful. However, as is the case, all things come to an end. When Frank was busted and facing life in prison, he flipped, turning states evidence for the Fed's bringing about the convictions of more than a hundred associates. It is important to note that most of those criminals were on the police force. His nefarious career was dramatized in the 2007 feature film "American Gangster."

Then there was the flamboyant Leroy "Nicky" Barnes, Mr. Untouchable, leader of the notorious African American crime organization known as "The Council". Seven powerful Harlem gangsters made up "The Council". It was organized similarly to the Mafia and controlled the rest of the heroin trade. Barnes was convicted in 1978 of multiple counts under the RICO (Racketeer Influenced and Corrupt Organizations) statute including drug trafficking and murder. He was sentenced to life in prison without eligibility for parole.

While in prison, Barnes too became a "rat" turning state's evidence against his former associates in The Council. In exchange for his testimony Barnes was released into the Federal Witness Protection Program. It could be said that there is no honor among thieves I suppose. Comparing the gangsters of the two era's one thing is clear – despite the viciousness of their chosen profession the contemporary gangster's careers were short-lived and all of their ill-gotten gains were lost.

What these characters did was no different from what the slave masters did. Through the distribution of drugs, they enriched themselves by making slaves of men and women; leaving Harlem with a drug addiction rate that was ten times higher than the New York City average and twelve times higher than in the United States as a whole.

Then, in the 1980's, a new plague fell upon Harlem as well as many other communities. The use of crack cocaine became widespread producing a scourge of collateral crime as addicts stole anything they could get their hands on to feed their habit. Dealers fought for the right to sell in particular regions or over deals gone bad causing the murder rate to skyrocket. By the end of the crack wars in the mid 90's and with the initiation of aggressive policing; crime in Harlem plummeted and a sense of normalcy returned to the once proud historical hamlet.

Boo I am proud to tell you that today, Harlem is being resurrected. Will it reach the level of its glorious past? I don't know if it will return to the days of its greater glory or if it will ever be called the "Capital of Black America" but it warms my heart to see that it might return to significant grandeur. What I do know is that its magnificent past will forever hold a place of prominence in the annals of time.

Chapter Sixteen

My grandson was watching me in a way that gave the impression that he was full of pride and pleased with the empowering history I shared. I'm sure he had never been taught the history of our past with such honesty. He asked, "Are there any more places like that Granddad?" "Sure son, every city or town had such a place" I replied.

There was a prominent Brownsville community in Baltimore. Boo immediately said, "I've been to Baltimore." This was one of the most affluent African American neighborhoods in the United States at the turn of the twentieth century. Let's journey to a place I'll call the "Jewel of the Chesapeake." Today, B-more is called "Charm City" which should have been the name given to this splendid community known as Upton back in the day.

In Upton, Pennsylvania Avenue was the main drag connecting all African American life in the city and beyond. To the south and west of Upton was the poor and working class African American neighborhood called "The Bottom." To its east were the German American and Jewish American neighborhoods. Upton was about a fifteen minute walk from downtown Baltimore. But, blacks of that era had no need to go downtown for obvious reasons; they were not allowed to patronize or enter through the front door of the white establishments, not even if they were working at that establishment.

Baltimore is best known for crabs, crab cakes, delicious seafood, and of course, a good time but let's never forget its rich history. Upton was home to the most educated African Americans, property owners and professionals. Its residents included doctors, lawyers and retailers who served the middle class and an upscale clientele. The Avenue, as it was called, was home to a premiere shopping strip for Black Baltimoreans that inspired comparisons to Lenox Avenue in Harlem. Upton had it all – jazz clubs, dance halls, theaters, as well as other public and private institutions for the black community.

It was a major staging ground for much of the local and national civil rights initiatives. It was a crossroad for many great African Americans who fought for equality, intent upon improving conditions for communities suffering from the rigid and cruel separate but equal laws. Great people like Frederick Douglass, Justice Thurgood Marshall, Booker T. Washington, W.E.B. Du Bois and Marcus Garvey visited Upton and organized in its churches. The Baltimore chapter of the NAACP was based in Upton as well as the New Negro Alliance; both of which rallied for justice from within this proud community.

My grandson interrupted me to ask, "What is the NAACP?" This was a huge shock for an African American child not to know the National Association for the Advancement of Colored People. "What have they done to the minds of this generation?" Well son let me tell you about the NAACP. It was founded Feb. 12. 1909. It is the largest and most widely recognized grassroots-based civil rights organization. It had more than a half-million members and supporters throughout the United States and the world. The organization is the premier advocates for civil rights and equal opportunity.

The NAACP fought and still fights discrimination. However, it's most notable achievement was the successful court case in the 1950's where it's Legal Defense and Educational Fund, headed by Thurgood Marshall, secured a verdict from the Supreme Court that outlawed segregation in public schools. This historic case, known as Brown v. Board of Education in 1954, changed the world. This was a huge step toward the eradication of segregation. It is because of this case that you can sit in your classroom with white children today.

Now, back to Upton, in the mid-20th century, Upton's population swelled due to the popularity of the neighborhood and the pressures of segregation that kept African Americans confined to certain areas. Single family homes were subdivided into small apartments. Pennsylvania Avenue's sidewalks were crowded on Saturday nights as loud music and heavy drinking became popular vices on the strip. There were several notable venues hosting great entertainment like the New Albert Hall, the Savoy and the Strands that drew many performers and party-goers.

But it was the Douglass Theater, renamed The Royal Theater, at Pennsylvania and Lafayette Avenues that became a famous mainstay on the Chitlin Circuit. Many have said, at that time, it was considered to be on par with the legendary Apollo Theater. "Have you ever heard of the Chitlin Circuit," I asked. My bright eyed grandson answered by asking, "What is that granddad?"

The Chitlin Circuit was the collective name given to the string of performance venues throughout the eastern and southern United States that were safe, acceptable, and in most cases, the only places Negro musicians, comedians, and other entertainers could perform during the segregated era. It was in these venues where the greats of the past crafted their skills and laid the foundation for the great performers who entertain us today.

The most popular of these venues were the Cotton Club, Wilt's Small Paradise, the famed Apollo Theater, Robert's Show Lounge, Club Delisa, the Regal Theatre in Chicago, the Howard Theater in Washington, DC, the Uptown Theater in Philadelphia, the Ritz Theater in Jacksonville, Florida, the Fox Theater in Detroit, the Victory Grill in Austin, Texas, the Hippodrome Theater in Richmond, and the Royal Theater here in Baltimore. It is with great pride and reverence that I honor the memory and contributions of these venues.

Boo said, "WOW granddad!" I was sure he had never heard of any of these places but I thought it was important to make him aware of them because this part of history has been erased from the minds of a generation. I was however proud that Boo excitedly looked on with great interest as I continue my quest to resurrect the ghosts of those storied segregated communities of a time long past.

Stars such as Ethel Waters, Pearl Bailey, Louis Armstrong, Fats Waller, James Brown, Stevie Wonder, the Temptations and the Jackson Five all performed at the Royal. It was like the Apollo in the sense that you had to play the Royal to get your chops. In fact, Cab Calloway grew up in Upton and Eubie Blake performed his debut in a club on Pennsylvania Avenue.

Churches were a huge part of this community providing safe havens for its people. Since the 18th century African American churches have nurtured souls, fed the hungry, clothed and housed the poor but their overall role was far more significant. From the beginning, going back beyond the Underground Railroad, Baltimore's churches were places of empowerment through worship.

The church was the backbone of the community serving as a communication network and they were used as a launch pad for activism. Just as it was from our origins in this country, our survival depended upon faith in something greater than ourselves. The church community fought for civil rights, supported business initiatives and job placement. They served as incubators for organizing and planning regardless of someone's denomination or faith.

Baltimore has produced prominent businessmen such as Raymond Haysbert who was the owner and founder of the famed Parks Sausage Company that became the first black-owned company to go public in 1969. The Parks Sausage Company was a legend in Baltimore and you could hear its slogan "more Parks Sausages Mom" everywhere. After the company experienced financial difficulties, two former National Football League Hall of Famers, Lydell Mitchell and Franco Harris, partnered to come to its rescue maintaining the company's black-owned legacy. James Brown, the "Godfather of Soul," was also a prominent businessman in the city owning the local radio station WEBB and several other businesses.

Upton also produced its share of legendary and colorful characters known as "hustlers". One of the most famous was "Little Willie" Adams. Mr. Adams, or "Little Willie" as he was known, opened a shoeshine stand on the Avenue when he was 18. Sources say he was an ambitious young hustler with dreams of being his own man. One day a flamboyant numbers man sat in his chair. He popped his rag like a firecracker while talking jive, making him laugh. He convinced the numbers man that he too was a businessman, solid and dependable, and that he wanted in on the numbers game. The hustlers slapped palms and Little Willie started at the bottom the next day as a runner.

Hustling was a family business and Little Willie was taught by his grandfather who ran an after-hours gambling house on Madison Avenue where most of Baltimore's established hustlers and entrepreneurs enjoyed their favorite vices. Little Willie was a welcomed star at grand pop's gambling house as he was eager to learn this way of life as early as age seven. By age 34, the young dapper Adams was already a living legend and the King of B-more. Little Willie was known to say, after he became the numbers czar, "This was our thing started by slaves." I'm told he would say that "prayer is good but when you get up off your knees, you've got to hustle."

Then there was Mr. Melvin Williams who was the inspiration for the enormously popular HBO series, "The Wire." Known as "Little Melvin," he was also featured in the documentary "American Gangster" where he told his story his way. Little Melvin, a legend at age 15, had made a few hundred grand in the gambling haunts and alleyways along glittering Pennsylvania Avenue before he was old enough to shave. Little Melvin possessed a genius I.Q. of 160 but he says it's closer to 200. Despite being a high school dropout he can talk tax codes, inner-state commerce, calculus and physics with the best of them.

In the 1960's when heroin addiction exploded in urban neighborhoods, Mafia drug traffickers sought out connections in big cities with people who were accustomed to dealing with large sums of cash and were smart enough to keep their mouths shut. They needed to look no further than to Little Melvin known in street lore today as the man who brought heroin to Baltimore and ruled the city's underworld as the uncrowned king for three decades.

Baltimore police were frustrated with their inability to penetrate his operation, so they framed him by planting a handful of pills in his pocket during an orchestrated bust. Five years later, Melvin emerged from prison a bitter man out for revenge. He accomplished his mission accumulating untold millions in narco-profits. But, ultimately, he paid the price for his eminence with a 26.5 year prison sentence.

His street legend was larger than life. When the Baltimore riots erupted after the murder of Dr. Martin Luther King, Jr.; city leaders came to Melvin's door on the fourth morning of fire and rage. In walked National Guard Gen. George Gelston, State Sen. Clarence Mitchell III, and Police Maj. William "Box" Harris. "We think you can help stop the rioting," they said. "We'll give you a bullhorn and a bullet-proof vest."

Williams showed his resolve and command of the streets telling them; "I'll take the bullhorn. Give the vest to Senator Mitchell." That afternoon, as thousands stood at Pennsylvania Avenue and Mosher Street, Williams told the crowd that they'd expressed their rage and they'd made their point; now it's time go home. The streets quickly emptied and that day the riots were over. This must have shocked the cities élite to know that this man had such power in there city.

In the 1960's and 70's controversial urban renewal projects destroyed much of Upton's historic architecture, especially in the southwestern portion of the neighborhood. However, only a portion of what was removed was actually replaced. Once the buildings were razed it was difficult to secure developers to build new construction. What pained many in Charm City was that the famed Royal Theater was demolished in 1971. Further problems faced Upton during this time in the form of economic depression, housing abandonment, crime and rioting.

Pennsylvania Avenue is now lined with sneaker shops, dollar stores, low-rent commercial entities, and abandoned storefronts. The Avenue Market sells produce and holds occasional events such as jazz shows. According to the city, 60% of Upton families with children under 5 live in poverty. Many of the row houses in the neighborhood are vacant; either abandoned by their property owners or owned by the city.

The ghost of what was our creation has been stained and the Jewel of the Chesapeake has lost its luster. Unfortunately, the city of Baltimore, known as Charm City, forgot that Upton was a large part of its charm but African Americans know that its legacy will never truly die.

I asked my grandson, "Do you remember yesterday when we went to Washington DC?" Boo answered, "Yes Granddad". There were many Brownsville's there too. Washington is the capital of the free world with its avenues of grand marble structures that are more or less a crystallization of magnificence for tourists to admire. The architectural marvels we saw yesterday are mere symbols of power associated with America's wealth.

Let me tell you about another Brownsville community in DC back in the day. Although, not common knowledge, it's rich African American history sadly has become little more than a footnote in the annals of time. You must understand that these segregated communities were the result of an unholy system imposed upon people of color but there greatness is part our proud history.

This place was what we now know as Georgetown. There is a hidden Washington that some call a tale of two cities. Just blocks from Washington's marbled symbols of opulence live the disenfranchised, downtrodden in neighborhoods of the forgotten. You see son, prior to 1967 the city was run by and under federal control, which is why it is called a District – i.e., the District of Columbia. It was President Johnson who appointed Walter Washington, an African American, as the city's first ever Mayor-Commissioner in an effort that came to be known as home rule.

The city has always been predominately African American with no real authority over its direction. The "District" as many locals call it was at that time a sleepy southern town not much different than a town in South Carolina or Mississippi as far as African Americans were concerned. It was run by Dixiecrats to this point and the Dixiecrats were worse than what we know today as Conservative Republicans who are the nucleus of the Republican Party. What you may not know – even today Washington has no voting representation in Congress - making the capital of the free world basically a plantation.

Washington has many African American enclaves that have long and storied histories but most do not know Georgetown, one of Washington's most renowned upscale communities, was once one of them. It is probably best known today as the home of Georgetown University with its championship basketball teams coached by the legendary John Thompson and now his son JT III who leads the basketball team. Many luminous basketball players in the NBA were produced by that institution.

Most people know Georgetown for its world renowned nightlife, shopping or the fact that it is home to many famous people. One of its most famous residents was a young John Kennedy, along with his new bride Jackie, called Georgetown home prior to moving into the White House. Today, Georgetown is home to many influential and prominent people. In fact, it is virtually a Who's Who of Washington power brokers who occupy Georgetown with little connection to its past heritage.

It is also worth mentioning that many notable African American figures resided in other segregated communities around town such as the great orator Fredrick Douglass who owned a home in Anacostia. Carter G. Woodson, creator of "Black History Month," owned a home in the Shaw neighborhood of the city. These great men and all prominent African American politicians, artists, entrepreneurs, scholars, athletes and socialites were relegated to live in a town divided by the harsh separate-but-equal laws of the day.

Georgetown began as a Maryland tobacco port on the banks of the Potomac River in 1751. When Congress created the District of Columbia to be the nation's capital in 1791, its 10-mile square boundaries were drawn to include this port town, as well as the very similar Virginia tobacco port of Alexandria just across the river. Alexandria was given back to Virginia in 1846 but Georgetown remained as one of Washington's most lively urban neighborhoods.

Georgetown historically had a large African American population, including both slaves and free blacks. Slave labor was widely used in the construction of new buildings in Washington just as they were used to provide labor on tobacco plantations in Maryland and Virginia. Let me be very clear, slave labor was the workforce that built Washington's opulent marble structures.

Georgetown was also a major slave trading depot, dating back to as early as 1760. John Beattie established a slave trading business on O Street and conducted business at other locations called "pens" around Wisconsin Avenue and M Street. Both locations were just a short distance from the White House. Slave trading continued until the mid-19th century when slavery ended in the city on April 16, 1862. Hence, many former slaves moved to Georgetown, establishing this thriving community following their freedom.

When African Americans settled in Georgetown, the freemen established the Mount Zion United Methodist Church that remains a prominent fixture there today. Prior to establishing the church, free blacks and slaves went to the Dumbarton Methodist Church where they were restricted to a hot overcrowded balcony. Mount Zion is the oldest African American congregation in Washington. In addition to providing a place of worship, the church provided a cemetery for free burials to Washington's earlier African American population.

This feat was due to their strong religious convictions and was a testament to their fortitude in spite of experiencing the horrors of slavery. I'm sure a sense of extreme pride was evident in Washington at the time because it became home to Howard University. Although not in Georgetown, this preeminent university was established for blacks in 1867 with the aid of the Freedmen's Bureau. It was named for the Commissioner of the Freedmen's Bureau General Oliver Otis Howard.

The Freedmen's Bureau was intended to help solve everyday problems of the newly freed slaves but its most widely recognized achievements were its accomplishments in the area of education. Prior to the Civil War no southern state had a system of universal state supported public education for "coloreds" but Washington now had an advanced school of learning.

In the early twentieth century new construction of large apartment buildings began to move into Georgetown. The eyes of the elite became trained on the area. John Ihlder led efforts to take advantage of new zoning laws to get restrictions enacted on construction in Georgetown. However, legislators largely ignored concerns about the historic preservation of Georgetown until 1950 when Public Law 808 was passed establishing the historic district of "Old Georgetown."

The law required the United States Commission of Fine Arts to be consulted on any alteration, demolition or building construction within the historic district. It was during this time that the Citizens Association of Georgetown was formed. As you can imagine, this proper and official sounding solution was not designed to benefit the African American citizens living in Georgetown. In fact, it is my understanding that the Old Georgetown Act was really a polite, or maybe not so polite, way of saying gentrification.

Georgetown began to emerge as the fashion and cultural center of the newly identified community. While many "old families" stayed in Georgetown the neighborhood's population became poorer and more racially diverse. Its demographics started to shift as a wave of new post war residents arrived with many politically savvy and well-educated people from elite backgrounds. They took a keen interest in the neighborhood's historic nature for their own benefit.

I am not implying nor suggesting that the Old Georgetown Act was designed to remove African Americans and poor residents from the community (wink), but it did create an environment where people of low to moderate income could no longer afford to live. High-end developments and gentrification have revitalized the formerly African American neighborhood. What was once viewed as a blighted industrial waterfront in now an elite white enclave.

The District's old refuse incinerator and smokestack preserved for years as an abandoned but historic landmark was redeveloped in 2003 to become part of the most pronounced feature of the Ritz-Carlton Hotel. This is what

I think happened in simple terms according to the thinking of the day: "the system is designed to protect the system". This was always the case when it came to us and to those who would benefit from us to accommodate the needs of those who control the system.

Chapter Seventeen

I was exuberant and as happy as any man could be while we sat at the dinner table knowing that I was giving my grandson wisdom that would enable him to know who he is deep within his soul. As any grandfather would say after spending time with his grandson; I've really enjoyed his company and another wonderful day. While serving my precious grandson his dinner he asked, "Granddad you have told me a lot about history but you have not talked about many people. Who were some of the black hero's and great people?"

"Boo there are many great people who have made valuable contributions to our story. I call them the ghost of the greats whose shoulders we stand". What is important to remember is that it is because of these champions of valor that we owe a debt of gratitude and we should honor them for all time. Just know that nearly everything you know and everything that ever was an African American played a role in its creation or influenced it. So it will be a pleasure to tell you about some of these great men, and women.

Alright, let me begin with Dr. Martin Luther King, the Prince of Peace, who was and is the most revered leader of our time. Dr. King's major accomplishments were the Montgomery Bus Boycott, being the founder and first President of the Southern Christian Leadership Conference, and the famed March on Washington. He was posthumously awarded the Presidential Medal of Freedom, the Congressional Gold Medal, a National Holiday, and will be honored with a monument on the Washington Mall. However, his most notable accomplishment was being the youngest person to receive the Nobel Peace Prize.

His legacy was secured through his efforts to sustain the progress of civil rights for Negro's and poor people that led him to become a human rights icon recognized as a martyr. He was born in Atlanta, Georgia on January 15, 1929 the son of the Reverend Martin Luther King, Sr. who was born "Michael King." Few people know that Martin Luther King, Jr. was originally named "Michael King, Jr." until the family traveled to Europe in 1934 visiting Germany. Soon after this trip the elder King changed both their names to Martin Luther in honor of the German Protestant leader Martin Luther.

King was originally skeptical of many Christian claims. Most striking perhaps was his denial of the bodily resurrection of Jesus during Sunday school at the age of thirteen. From this point he stated, "Doubts began to spring forth unrelentingly." However, throughout his career of service, he wrote and spoke frequently, drawing on his experience as a preacher, which he understood to be his purpose. For example, in his "letter from Birmingham Jail," written in 1963 is a passionate testament to his crusade for justice.

Dr. King first appeared on the national scene as the leader of the Montgomery Bus Boycott. We have been taught to believe that Mrs. Parks' refusal to give up her seat that day was an anomaly. The fact is many blacks refused, at one time or another, to give up their seats in the white only section usually resulting in being run out of town. However, there was a committee in place silently waiting for an instance where they could take it through the legal system to put an end to this unholy system of segregation.

For example, in March 1955 a fifteen-year-old school girl, Claudette Colvin refused to give up her bus seat to a white man in compliance with the Jim Crow Laws. King was on the committee from the Birmingham African American community that looked into the case. But the committee decided to wait for a better case to pursue. It was on December 1, 1955 the case they were waiting for appeared.

Mrs. Rosa Parks was arrested for refusing to give up her seat that resulted in the Montgomery Bus Boycott, planned by E. D. Nixon and led by Dr. King emerged. The boycott lasted for 385 days crippling the city economically. The situation became so tense that King's house was bombed and he was arrested during this campaign. The case ultimately ended with a United States District Court ruling in Browder v. Gayle that ended racial segregation on all Montgomery public buses and throughout the south.

History will most remember Dr. King for his famous "I have a dream speech" during the monumental March on Washington for Jobs and Freedom that took place on August 28, 1963. Dr. King, representing SCLC, was among the leaders of the so-called "Big Six" civil rights organizations who were instrumental in organizing this massive event. The other leaders and organizations comprising the Big Six were Roy Williams from the NAACP, Whitney Young of the Urban League, A. Philip Randolph of the Brotherhood of Sleeping Car Porters, John Lewis of SNCC, and James Farmer of the Congress of Racial Equality with King's colleague Bayard Rustin being the primary logistical and strategic organizer.

The march originally was conceived as an event to dramatize the desperate condition of blacks. This was supposed to be a very public opportunity to place their grievances squarely before the seat of power in the nation's capital. King's leadership role caused a controversy because he was one of the key figures who acceded to the wishes of President Kennedy in changing the focus of the march. It is a fact that Kennedy initially opposed the march outright. He was concerned it would negatively impact the drive for passage of civil rights legislation but the organizers stood their ground concerning the march.

The organizers firmly intended to challenge the federal government for its failure to safeguard the civil rights of Negro's in this country. After King gave his "I Have a Dream" speech during the March on Washington, the FBI described King as "the most dangerous and effective Negro leader in the country." In December 1963, FBI officials were gathered for a special conference and alleged that King was "knowingly, willingly and regularly cooperating with and taking guidance from communists" whose long-term strategy was to create a "Negro-labor" coalition detrimental to American security.

The attempt to prove that King was a Communist reflected the feeling of many segregationists that blacks in the South were happy with their lot. They believed the march was being stirred up by "communists" and "outside agitators." The civil rights movement arose from activism within the black community long before World War I. In response to the FBI's comments regarding communists directing the civil rights movement King said, "The Negro revolution is a genuine revolution, born from the same womb that produces all massive social upheavals, the womb of intolerable conditions and unendurable situations."

Starting in 1965, King began to express doubts about the United States' role in the Vietnam War. In an April 4, 1967 appearance at the Riverside Church in New York, exactly one year before his death, King delivered a speech titled "Beyond Vietnam." In that speech, he spoke strongly against the United States' role in the war insisting that the U.S. was in Vietnam "to occupy it as an American colony". He went further calling the U.S. government "the greatest purveyor of violence in the world today."

Dr. King also was opposed to the war on the grounds that the war took money and resources that could have been spent on social welfare services like the War on Poverty. I am positive if Dr. King were here today he would say the same thing with regard to the current wars we have no business fighting. At the time of his death, April 4, 2011, Dr. King was working on a second March on Washington called a "Poor Peoples March". Unfortunately, before the march was realized Dr. King went to Memphis, Tennessee in support of black sanitary workers who had been on strike for higher wages and better treatment.

On April 3, Dr. King addressed a rally and delivered his "I've Been to the Mountaintop" address at Mason Temple, which was the world headquarters of the Church of God in Christ. This speech is viewed by many as the most prophetic speech ever delivered. It is ironic that Dr. King's flight to Memphis had been delayed by a bomb threat against his plane. Yet, he persevered. Dr. King was assassinated the next evening on the balcony of the Lorraine Motel.

King's wife, Coretta Scott King, followed in her husband's footsteps after his death and was active in matters of social justice and civil rights until her death in 2006. The same year that Martin Luther King was assassinated she established the King Center in Atlanta, Georgia dedicated to preserving his legacy and the work of championing non-violent conflict resolution and tolerance worldwide. We are blessed that Dr. King was allowed to walk among us and that he had the moral aptitude to change the world.

Boo what you need to know is that there is a myth that Dr. King only had a dream because most have forgotten the main message of the famous "I have a Dream Speech". True; he did say those words. However, putting the speech in context the main message of the speech was to tell the world that America had not for filled its promise to Negro's and the poor. He clearly articulated during the speech that America had a debt that it had not paid and a check that had not been cashed. In my opinion his most memorable quote was: "Free at last, thank God almighty, we free at last". I hope that someday we will all be free.

We can thank Rosa Louise McCauley Parks for giving us the genius of Dr. King. Mrs. Parks is the most distinguished African American woman Civil Rights Activist of our time. The woman known as "the first lady of civil rights" was born February 4, 1913 in Tuskegee, Alabama to James McCauley and Leona Edwards a carpenter and a teacher, respectively. Her ancestry was a mixture of African American, Cherokee-Creek and Scots-Irish, which some say accounts for her fair complexion.

His-Story wants us to believe this act was the first of its kind in the rigidly segregated south but it was not the first of its kind. Lest we forget that in 1944 athletic star Jackie Robinson took a similar stand in a confrontation with a US Army officer in Texas refusing to move to the back of a bus. Robinson was brought before a court martial for this act of disobedience and was acquitted. The NAACP had accepted and litigated other cases, such as that of Irene Morgan ten years earlier, which resulted in a victory in the U.S. Supreme Court on grounds related to the Interstate Commerce Clause. The difference as it relates to the many individuals whose arrests for civil disobedience was that Mrs. Parks' actions sparked the Montgomery Bus Boycott.

Son you must remember that Jim Crow was the law of the land with black and white people segregated in virtually every aspect of daily life and not just in the South. Bus and train companies did not provide separate vehicles for the different races but enforced seating policies that allocated separate sections for blacks and whites. School bus transportation was unavailable in any form for black school children in the South.

In Mrs. Parks' autobiography she recounts some of her earliest memories about the kindness of white strangers but because of her race she found it impossible to ignore racism. When the KKK marched down the street in front of her house she recalls her grandfather guarding the front door with a shotgun. The Montgomery Industrial School, founded and staffed by white northerners for black children, was burned twice by arsonist, i.e. the Klan, and its faculty was ostracized by the white community. What Mrs. Parks did was proved that just one person and one single act can change the world.

These are probably the most well-known of the Civil Rights icons but there were thousands who contributed to the struggle. My personal hero and the most significant unsung voice of our time was John Henrik Clarke. He was one of the most profoundly brilliant and empowering educators, in my opinion, to ever live. What is significant about Mr. Clarke is that he did the necessary and tedious organizing work to bring volumes of our true history into existence.

Thereby, offering an alternative outlook from the dominant mainstream views of such figures as Malcolm X and Nat Turner both of whom were often characterized as militant hate mongers. Clarke understood the necessity for us to affirm our belief in and respect both leaders. It is interesting that Clarke's work did not simply focused on investigating history as the past; rather proactively involving it with history in the making.

As a historian Mr. Clarke edited a books on Marcus Garvey, "Africa, Lost and Found" (with Richard Moore and Keith Baird), and "African People at the Crossroads". Two seminal historical works widely used in History and African American Studies on college and university campuses. Through the United Nations, he published monographs on Paul Robeson and W.E.B. DuBois. As an activist-historian, he produced the monograph Christopher

Columbus and the African Holocaust. His final published book was "Who Betrayed the African Revolution?" Which is a must read!

Now, in my opinion Malcolm X was no doubt one of the most profoundly significant, famous, and controversial African American leaders ever. I cannot recall any other MAN, except maybe Dr. King, whose impact was so overwhelmingly felt among people all over the world. The Minister's prophetic words spoken over forty-five years ago are as relevant today as the day they were spoken evoking the same emotions of truth.

Minister Malcolm X was assassinated February 21st, 1965 at the Audubon Ballroom. His murder has yet to be fully resolved in the minds of most of us nor though the criminal justice system. There were two maybe three men who were imprisoned for the crime but most doubt they were the killers. What I can say is that we lost a champion unlike any other who came before him. Therefore, it would be blasphemy not to include the most articulate orator in my lifetime.

I could go deeper into the making of this man but so many people, agencies, institutions and organizations have covered this great man's brief life on earth in much more detail than I can. There is a vast sea of in-depth analyses, books, movies, and biographies on his life and philosophies. I will not try to rewrite history, rather simply pay homage to the legacy of this great man as brief as I can; honoring him for his contributions to the African American Diaspora.

There are facts known and unknown, suspicions, and theories surrounding the assassination of Malcolm X with regard to the impact it's had on our culture and the world. Like the Reverend Dr. Martin Luther King, Malcolm X also had a dream. It began bathed in the tenets of anger and hatred fostered by economic independence on the shoulders of retaliatory separatism that ended with the swelling acceptance of a unified brotherhood. However, as his life ended that premise was replaced with peace and with the nagging thirst for international equality for all mankind.

The eulogy that actor Ossie Davis delivered at his funeral profoundly impresses upon us that "However we may have differed with him, or with each other about him and his value as a man, let his going from us serve only to bring us together, now. Consigning these mortal remains to earth, the common mother of all, secure in the knowledge that what we place in the ground is no more now a man but a seed which, after the winter of our discontent, will come forth again to meet us. And we will know him then for what he was and is a Prince, our own black shining Prince! Who didn't hesitate to die, because he loved us so."

Today, Malcolm X is known in America and throughout the world with reverence. He was a celebrated freedom fighter and a motivating force to those whose future he had the vision to see and the will to stand up and fight for justice. Postage stamps and posters now bear his image out of recognition and honor for his final crusade. Malcolm X was a man who fulfilled his place in history and stayed true to his words: *"It is a time for martyrs now, and if I am to be one, it will be for the cause of brotherhood."* Rest in Peace.

When you talk about great African American's my personal hero must be included at the top of the list - Muhammad Ali, born Cassius Marcellus Clay, Jr. He is universally known as the "Greatest of All Times". Ali is called "The Greatest" because he is widely considered the greatest heavyweight boxers of all time. After turning professional, he went on to become the first and only boxer to win the lineal heavyweight championship three times and for being involved in several historic boxing matches. Notable among these are three with rival Joe Frazier and one with George Foreman whom he beat by knockout to win the world heavyweight title for the second time.

Ali changed his name after joining the Nation of Islam in 1964 subsequently converting to Sunni Islam in 1975. In 1967, Ali refused to be conscripted into the U.S. military based on his religious beliefs and opposition to the Vietnam War. He was arrested, found guilty on draft evasion charges, stripped of his boxing title, and his boxing license was suspended. He was not imprisoned but did not fight again for nearly four years while his appeal worked its way up to the U.S. Supreme Court where it was successful.

Ali was well known for his unorthodox fighting style, which he described as "float like a butterfly, sting like a bee" employing techniques such as the rope-a-dope. He was best known for his pre-match hype where he would "trash talk" to his opponents on television and in person before a match, often with rhymes. These personality quips and idioms along with an unorthodox fighting technique made him a cultural icon.

After winning the championship from Liston in 1964, Clay revealed that he was a member of the Nation of Islam, often called the Black Muslims, and the Nation gave Clay the name Cassius X, discarding his surname as a symbol of his ancestors' enslavement as had been done by other Nation members. On Friday, March 6, 1964, Elijah Muhammad recorded a statement over the phone to be played over the radio that Clay would be renamed Muhammad (one who is worthy of praise) Ali (fourth rightly guided caliph).

The Champ will be however remembered for his defiant stance concerning the Vietnam War. He declared that he would not serve in the United States Army and publicly considered himself a conscientious objector. Ali stated that "War is against the teachings of the Holy Qur'an. I'm not trying to dodge the draft. We are not supposed to take part in no wars unless declared by Allah or The Messenger. We don't take part in Christian wars or wars of any unbelievers." Ali also famously said in 1966: "I ain't got no quarrel with them Viet Cong ... They never called me nigger."

For refusing his scheduled induction into the U.S. Armed Forces on April 28, 1967 in Houston was a felony punishable by five years in prison and a fine of $10,000. As a result, he was arrested and on the same day the New York State Athletic Commission suspended his boxing license and stripped him of his title as did other boxing commissions. At the trial on June 20, 1967, after only 21 minutes of deliberation, the jury found Ali guilty. After a Court of Appeals upheld the conviction the case went to the U.S. Supreme Court.

During this time, the public began turning against the war and support for Ali began to grow. Ali supported himself by speaking at colleges and universities across the country where opposition to the war was especially strong. On June 28, 1971, the Supreme Court reversed his conviction for refusing induction by unanimous decision in Clay v. United States. The decision was not based on, nor did it address, the merits of Clay's/Ali's claims per se; rather the Government's failure to specify which claims were rejected and which were sustained constituted the grounds upon which the Court reversed the conviction.

During a time when Negroes dared to speak the Champ spoke loudly and for those with no voice. He made these two profound statements after he refused induction: "Why should they ask me to put on a uniform and go ten thousand miles from home and drop bombs and bullets on brown people in Vietnam while so-called Negro people in Louisville are treated like dogs and denied simple human rights?" The Champ also made this powerful statement: "No, I am not going 10,000 miles to help murder, kill and burn other people to simply help continue the domination of white slave masters over dark people the world over." Ali is the most recognized man in the world, revered by all, and the "Champ" for life.

Boo you are going to love this woman, she is the famous heroine sometimes referred to as "Moses." Harriett Tubman is, in my opinion, the most courageous woman during our struggle and my personal female hero. The tiny "dash" on her life's final marker says she was the great conductor of the Underground Railroad, a scout, spy, and nurse during the Civil War. In my opinion, it should contain a simple inscription that says – "Servant of God."

She was born Araminta Ross, however the date of her actual birth is suspect because as a slave accurate birth records were not kept. Therefore, no one can say for sure as to the actual date. She always proclaimed her birth as 1825 but most historians believe she was born around 1820 or 1821. Boo you might want to know she was born, lived, and did her greatest work just up the road from where you live.

After escaping from slavery into which she was born. She made thirteen missions to rescue over seventy slaves using the network of antislavery activists and safe houses known as the Underground Railroad. She once remarked that "she could have saved a lot more, if they had only known they were slaves." Her courage was that of unimaginable proportions because death was the penalty for such work.

One of her last missions into Maryland was to retrieve her aging parents. Her father, Ben, had purchased Rit, her mother in 1855 from Eliza Brodess for twenty dollars. Two years later, Tubman received word that her father had harbored a group of eight escaped slaves and was at risk of arrest. She traveled to the Eastern Shore and led them north into Canada.

In fact, it was believed by the late 1850's, the white abolitionist John Brown was suspected of secretly enticing slaves away from the Eastern Shore before his ill-fated raid on Harper's Ferry. Tubman was introduced to the insurgent John Brown who advocated the use of violence to destroy slavery. Although she never advocated violence against whites she agreed with his course of direct action and supported his goals. Like Tubman, he spoke of being called by God and trusted the divine to protect him from the wrath of slaveholders. She claimed to have had a prophetic vision prior to meeting Brown before their encounter.

Tubman did help Brown as he began recruiting supporters for an attack on slaveholders. Brown referred to her as "General Tubman." Her knowledge of support networks and resources in the border states of Pennsylvania, Maryland and Delaware was invaluable to Brown and his planners. She was unlike Frederick Douglass, William Lloyd Garrison, and other abolitionists who did not endorse his tactics. Tubman was for the end of slavery by any means necessary.

Brown dreamed of fighting to create a new state for freed slaves and made preparations for military action. He thought, after the first battle slaves would rise up and carry out a rebellion across the south. He asked Tubman to gather former slaves who might be willing to join his fighting force, which she did. Tubman was busy during this time giving talks to abolitionist audiences and tending to her relatives causing her to be unaware of the actual attack.

Thankfully, in the autumn of 1859 as Brown and his men prepared to launch the attack on Harpers Ferry - Tubman was not present. The raid failed. Brown was convicted of treason and hung in December. His actions were seen by abolitionists as a symbol of proud resistance carried out by a noble martyr. Tubman herself was effusive with praise. She later told a friend: "He done more in dying than 100 men would in living."

As Tubman aged, the sleeping spells and suffering from her childhood head trauma continued to plague her. By 1911, her body was so frail that she had to be admitted into the rest home named in her honor. A New York newspaper described her as "ill and penniless," prompting supporters to offer a new round of donations. Surrounded by friends and family members Harriet Tubman died of pneumonia on March 10, 1913. Just before she died, she told those in the room: "I go to prepare a place for you."

In the early twentieth century a new movement was afoot called Pan-Africanist. W.E.B Dubois was a pioneer of this movement. He was a profound intellectual and one of the unsung thinkers of our time. He was a man memorialized by the few who understood his genius and neglected by the many that were afraid of his loquacious espousals would unite the oppressed throughout the world into revolution.

His government name was William Edward Burghardt Dubois who was known as a man of spirited devotion and scholarly dedication. He was often called an attacker of injustice and a defender of freedom. Dubois was a forerunner of Black Nationalism and Pan-Africanism. He died in self-imposed exile in his home away from home with his ancestors of a glorious past – Africa. Dr. Dubois was labeled a "radical" ignored by those who hoped that his massive contributions would be buried alongside him. I say they should have listened.

Then there was Ralph Johnson Bunche, a man seldom mention but another great man nonetheless. He was born in Detroit, Michigan. His enduring fame arises from his service to the U. S. government and to the UN as an adviser to the Department of State, a military advisor on Africa and colonial areas of strategic military importance during World War II.

Bunche moved from his first position as an analyst in the Office of Strategic Services to the desk of acting chief of the Division of Dependent Area Affairs in the State Department. He also discharged various responsibilities in connection with international conferences of the Institute of Pacific Relations, the UN, the International Labor Organization, and the Anglo-American Caribbean Commission.

Then there was the man who came to be the last survivor of the "Big Four" James Farmer, the great debater, a principal founder of the Congress of Racial Equality; who shaped the civil-rights struggle in the United States in the mid-1950's and 60's. Farmer played a towering role in the movement as a direct-action leader of the organization popularly known as CORE and the most courageous freedom fighter of them all. Although attention in recent years focused on Dr. King's activities Farmer was a giant.

Claude Sitton, who covered the South for The New York Times during the civil rights struggle, observed:

"CORE under Farmer often served as the razor's edge of the movement. It was to CORE that the four Greensboro, N.C., students turned after staging the first in the series of sit-ins that swept the South in 1960. It was CORE that forced the issue of desegregation in interstate transportation with the Freedom Rides of 1961. It was CORE's James Chaney, Andrew Goodman and Michael Schwerner — a black and two whites — who became the first fatalities of the Mississippi Freedom Summer of 1964."

Let us never forget James Chaney, Andrew Goodman and Michael Schwerner who were murdered by a gang of Klansmen and buried beneath an earthen dam near the town of Philadelphia, Mississippi. These three martyrs deserve as much homage as any for making the ultimate sacrifice during the civil rights movement. They were more than hero's in the fight for freedom. These courageous men should be highly praised for all times. May their souls Rest in Peace.

I could not forgive myself if I neglected to talk about the genius of John Hope Franklin, a scholar and a towering historian, who helped create the field of African American history. He was a leading figure for nearly six decades. Dr. Franklin was a graduate of Fisk University. He received the A.M. and Ph.D. degrees in history from Howard University. He was the James B. Duke Professor Emeritus of History and for seven years the Professor of Legal History in the Law School at Duke University. He received more than 130 honorary degrees.

He taught at a number of institutions, including Fisk University, St. Augustine's College, North Carolina Central University, and Howard University. In 1956 he went to Brooklyn College as Chairman of the Department of History. In 1964, he joined the faculty of the University of Chicago serving as Chairman of the Department of History from 1967 to 1970. At Chicago, he was the John Matthews Manly Distinguished Service Professor from 1969 to 1982 where he became Professor Emeritus.

The grandson of a slave, Franklin was educated by his first-hand experience with injustices of racism, and not just in Rentiesville, Okla., but in the small black community where he was born on Jan. 2, 1915 and throughout his life. Named after John Hope, the former president of Atlanta University, Franklin was the son of Buck Colbert Franklin, one of the first black lawyers in the Oklahoma Indian territory and Mollie Parker Franklin, a schoolteacher and community leader.

In a statement to the American Academy of Arts and Letters in 2002 Franklin summed up his own career: "More than 60 years ago, I began the task of trying to write a new kind of Southern History. It would be broad in its reach, tolerant in its judgments of Southerners, and comprehensive in its inclusion of everyone who lived in the region. The long, tragic history of the continuing black-white conflict compelled me to focus on the struggle that has affected the lives of the vast majority of people in the United States. ... Looking back, I can plead guilty of having provided only a sketch of the work I laid out for myself."

Now, this man is often overlooked but never forgotten. Medgar Wiley Evers was the first martyr of the Civil Rights movement. He was born in Decatur, Mississippi on July 2, 1925; dying the victim of a racially motivated assassination on June 12, 1963 in Jackson, Mississippi after attending a rally. He was the third of four children of a small farm owner who also worked at a nearby sawmill. His social standing was impressed upon him every day; meaning to know his place. But Evers was determined not to cave in under such pressure. He once said his mission was evident at the age eleven or twelve when a close friend of the family was lynched.

Evers walked twelve miles each way to earn his high school diploma and joined the Army during the Second World War. Perhaps it was during those years of fighting in both France and Germany for other countries' freedom that convinced Evers to fight on his own shores for the freedom of blacks. After serving honorably in the World War II he began working for the National Association for the Advancement of Colored People (NAACP) in 1952. He travelled throughout the state of Mississippi trying to encourage voter registration and worked tirelessly to enforce federally mandated integration laws.

On 12 June 1963, hours after President John F. Kennedy gave a televised speech condemning segregation, Evers was shot in the back with a high-powered rifle while returning home. He crawled into the house collapsing in front of his wife and three children; he died an hour later. The rifle that was found at the scene belonged to Byron De La Beckwith, a member of the all-white Citizens' Council, a statewide group opposed to racial integration akin to the KKK. Beckwith was tried twice but both trials ended with a hung jury and he was released.

Nearly thirty years later, thanks to the persistence of Evers' widow, Myrlie Evers-Williams, the case was reopened and Beckwith was tried and convicted in 1994. The conviction was upheld by the state supreme court in 1997. Evers-Williams published "For Us, The Living" in 1967. Beckwith's trial was the basis for the 1996 film "Ghosts of Mississippi" that starred Whoopi Goldberg.

Fannie Lou Hamer was another proud activist who was willing to die for our right to vote. She was born Fannie Lou Townsend who was also known as the lady who was "sick and tired of being sick and tired". She was born October 6, 1917 in Montgomery County, Mississippi the granddaughter of slaves. Coming from a family of sharecroppers, which was a condition not all that different from slavery. She was the youngest child in her family of 19 brothers and sisters.

Hamer was an inspirational figure to many involved in the struggle for civil rights. In 1962, at age 44, members of the Student Nonviolent Coordinating Committee (SNCC) volunteers came to town to hold a voter registration meeting. She was surprised to learn that African Americans actually had a constitutional right to vote. When SNCC members asked for volunteers to go to the courthouse to register to vote Fannie Lou was the first to raise her hand. This was a dangerous decision. She later reflected, "The only thing they could do to me was to kill me and it seemed like they'd been trying to do that a little bit at a time ever since I could remember."

When Hamer and others went to the courthouse they were jailed and beaten savagely by the police almost to the point of death. After her release she needed more than a month to recover. Though the incident had profound physical and psychological effects she returned to Mississippi to organize voter registration drives. This was to include the "Freedom Ballot Campaign", which was a mock election in 1963 to prepare for the "Freedom Summer" initiative in 1964. She was known to the volunteers of Freedom Summer, most of whom were young white and from northern states, as a motherly figure who believed that the civil rights effort should be multi-racial in nature. Hamer was the shoulders for the souls of the movement.

Frederick Augustus Washington Bailey, who later became known as Frederick Douglass, was the most eloquent orator of his day. He was an American icon for right, a social reformer, writer, and statesman after escaping slavery becoming a leader in the abolitionist movement. Douglass was renowned for his dazzling oratory and incisive antislavery writing. A firm believer in equality for all people regardless of race, color, or creed was fond of saying "I would unite with anybody to do right and with nobody to do wrong."

Boo this man was also born near your town. He was born a slave in Talbot County, Maryland in his grandmother's shack west of the Tuckahoe

Creek. He was separated from his mother, Harriet Bailey, when he was still an infant and lived with his maternal grandmother Betty Bailey. His mother died when Douglass was about seven and the identity of his father is obscure. However, he once claimed that he was told his father was a white man, perhaps his master Aaron Anthony, although later in his life he would say that he knew nothing of his father's identity.

He was acquainted with the radical abolitionist John Brown but disapproved of Brown's plan to start an armed slave rebellion in the south. Brown visited Douglass' home two months before he led the raid on the federal in Harpers Ferry in an effort to gain his support. After the raid, Douglass fled for a time to Canada fearing guilt by association and arrest as a co-conspirator. Douglass believed the attack on federal property would enrage the American public. Douglass later shared a stage at a speaking engagement in Harpers Ferry with the prosecutor who successfully convicted Brown.

Douglass conferred with President's Abraham Lincoln and Andrew Johnson concerning the treatment of black soldiers and on the subject of black suffrage. Douglass's support of the Civil War and believed it would provided all that was necessary to gain the freedom of African Americans and guarantee their rights. Douglass and the abolitionists argued because the aim of the Civil War was to end slavery, which he believed was why Negro's should be allowed to engage in the fight for their freedom. Douglass publicized this view in his newspapers and several speeches.

With the signing of the Emancipation Proclamation on January 1, 1863 declaring freedom for all slaves in Confederate held territory. It is worth noting that "slaves in Union held in the Northern states were not included in the Emancipation Proclamation". They would not become freed until the passage of the 13th Amendment on December 6, 1865. Douglass described the spirit of those awaiting the proclamation: "We were waiting and listening as for a bolt from the sky...we were watching...by the dim light of the stars for the dawn of a new day...we were longing for the answer to the agonizing prayers of centuries" and we continue to wait!

I could go on forever telling you about the ghost of the greats. But I will stop here with Marcus Mosiah Garvey a visionary and a manipulator, a brilliant orator and a pompous autocrat. He was best known as founder of the "Back to Africa Movement". Garvey was born in Jamaica and immigrated to Harlem in 1916 at the age of 28. While in his homeland, he admired Booker T. Washington's philosophy of self-improvement for people of African descent. Garvey formed the Jamaica Improvement Association.

Shortly after arriving in America his ideas expanded and he became a Black Nationalist. Garvey formed the Universal Negro Improvement Association (U.N.I.A) and became the first African American leader in American history to organize masses of people in a political movement. The Black Star Line shipping company and the Negro Factories Corporation were to be the commercial arms of the Garvey's movement. The Black Star Line failed because of purported mismanagement and lack of sufficient funds gave Garvey's enemies their chance to destroy him.

Investments in the line were lost. He was convicted of mail fraud and imprisoned in 1925. After serving 2 years 10 months of a 5-year sentence he was deported to Jamaica. His plans for colonization in Liberia had been sabotaged by colonial powers that brought pressure to bear on the Liberian government. As a result, the land which had been granted to the Garvey organization for the settlement overseas in Africans was given to the white American industrialist Harvey Firestone. The expensive equipment shipped to Liberia for Garvey's colonists was seized.

In emphasizing the need to have separate black institutions under black leadership Garvey anticipated the mood and thinking of the future black nationalists by nearly 50 years. He died, as he lived, an unbending apostle of African nationalism. Garvey left a legacy of racial pride and identification with a glorious African heritage. The symbols which he made famous, the Black Star of Africa and the red, black, and green flag of African liberation continue to inspire younger generations of African nationalists. Boo never forget these powerful words Garvey left for us: "Up! You mighty race; you can accomplish what you will."

What do you think of Black History and our hero's now? I have told you – he stopped me "No learned me granddad". With a big smile I said, "Sorry Boo. You are so right - learned you. These are just some of the things you should know about our courageous past and the people whose strong broad shoulders we stand." There are many pages of America history that are embedded in the "Founding of America". I want you to remember that Black History is American History and understand that His-Story's view of African American history was that "we are a nation of people living within a nation without a nationality".

Chapter Eighteen

"Granddad this has been the best week ever. I will never forget what you've taught me." I reminded him, "You mean learn you don't you?" "I was testing you granddad", he replied with a big smile. "Granddad I think you're the greatest. You made a book. Would you tell me about you?" "What do you want to know about me Boo?" He asked, "Would you read from your book and tell me about my dad?" I look at him with nothing but pride responding the only way I could – "yes, of course I will".

The experiences of my life sometimes felt like I had a halo over my head for all the good I've done and one day it felt like a noose around my neck. I started with nothing and out of nothing I found a way out of no way. So I have come to believe each day is a day that God made for me. You see son all God gave us was "*Just a Season*" and your dad gave me you who dictates the rhythm my soul. He brings me a copy of the novel and I begin to read the dedication to those I love:

As we travel through this existence I will call the evolution of life, people come into our lives only but for a moment. Through God's grace, I was blessed with the good fortune or privilege to have had many precious moments. Therefore, I am extremely proud and honored to have dedicated "Just a Season" to the loving memories of my wonderful Grandfather, Sylvanus Reed, my beloved Grandmother, Gladys Reed, and my precious son, your Dad, Rashad Ali Wills. I am confident that God has highly exalted each of them, as they rest peacefully for eternity.

When I think about what each has contributed to my life, it is a lot like adding ingredients to a wholesome stew. My grandfather, the greatest man I've ever known, instilled the ingredients of strength, leadership, direction, and common sense. While my loving Grandmother, my sweetheart, added the unique gifts of fortitude, tenacity, bravery, and the compassion within my soul, along with a big chunk of love. My son came into my life giving it the special ingredients of pride, gratitude, pleasure, and pain. By adding these ingredients to life's experiences, I was provided with the wisdom to live a dream.

Their inspiration, courage, and motivation humble me, and I'm filled with gratitude that their example enriched my soul before they made their transition into the kingdom of heaven. So much so that in those times of trouble, when the bridges are hard to cross and the road gets rough, I hear my Grandfather's gentle voice reciting words once spoken by the Prophet Isaiah: "Fear not for I am with you." And like my grandfather I say to him "Fear not for I am with you." Boo I will tell you, just as he told me, that I am with you.

I begin to read the prelude: A season is a time characterized by a particular circumstance, suitable to an indefinite period of time associated with a divine phenomenon that some call life. One of the first things I learned in this life was that it is a journey. During this passage through time I have come to realize that there are milestones, mountains, and valleys that everyone will encounter. Today, I have to face a valley and it's excruciating. It's June 28th, a day that I once celebrated as a very special day. Now, it's filled with sorrow. The reason this day is different from all others is because I have come to the cemetery at Friendly Church.

Normally it's hot and humid as summer begins, but not so today. It's a cool gray day with the sky slightly overcast. I hear the echo of birds chirping from a distance. There is also a mist or a light fog hovering very near the ground that gives the aura of a mystical setting. This is a place where many of my family members who have passed away rest for eternity. Some have been resting here for over a hundred years. I have grandparents, uncles, aunts, cousins, a sister, and many friends here as well. The cemetery is in the most tranquil of places secluded from the rest of the world, very peaceful and beautiful, almost like being near the gateway of heaven.

My heart aches today because I have come here on what would have been my son's birthday. This is a very hard thing for me to do as the natural order suggests it should be the other way around. Another difficulty is that this is the first time I will see his headstone that was put in place just a few days ago. Although I know what it should look like, it's going to be hard to actually see it. It will indicate the finality of losing the dearest of all human beings. It's hard to imagine what the rest of my life will be like without my precious son.

As I pass Granddaddy's gravesite, I stop to say hello. After a brief moment, I continue in the direction of my son's resting place. As I get closer, I begin to receive a rush of emotion to the point that my movements slow as the sight comes into view. I can now see his name clearly and I whisper "God why did you take him?" I become numb as I finally arrive at his gravesite, overwhelmed with this never before known emotion. This is something I never thought I would ever have to do, but here I am!!!

Suddenly, the sky begins to clear somewhat, as I now feel the sun's rays from above. At this very moment, I receive an epiphany upon reading the dates inscribed on the stone. 1981 – 2001. What does this really mean? The beginning and the end, surely, but in the final analysis it is just a tiny little dash that represents the whole life of a person. I fall to my knees realizing the profound impact of that thought causing me to look to the heavens and wonder. If someone, for whatever reason, were to tell the story concealed within my dash. What might they say? As I continued to read I could see my grandson swell with pride.

It's been said, there are no words that have not been spoken and there are no stories that have never been told but there are some that you will never forget. Your Granddad's life, as told in "Just a Season", is a luminous story into the life of a man who, in the midst of pain and loss, journeys back in time to reexamine all the important people, circumstances, and intellectual fervor that contributed to the richness of his life.

The story begins with me, a grief-stricken father, visiting the grave site of my beloved son, your father, who was killed in a tragic accident; a moment that no loving parent should ever have to face. As I sadly gaze at my son's headstone and read what is inscribed there, the dates 1981 - 2001 brings about an illuminating discovery. The tiny dash that separates the years of one's birth and death represents the whole of a person's life. So if this tiny dash were to tell my life's story, what would it say?

I could see his eye brighten immensely with enthusiasm as I empower him with the story that was written by someone greater than myself. After reading for about an hour I get to the part where his father came to be and my grandson seems to settle into a gentle calm. I wonder if it was because thing are revealed that he never knew. Like how special his dad was or simply knowing about us gave him peace. After all he was affected as much, if not more than anyone else by the death of Jarad. My heart begins to ach as I feel the pain of his pain, not having the opportunity to know his dad.

It's comforting and painful to share my story that includes telling him about his father. I want to make sure this child remembers his dad in spite of not knowing him. Then came the hardest part; reading the part where I brought my son home to rest at Friendly Church. It still seems a little odd because it still hurts so much when I have to relive this part of the story. Somehow, Boo must have known that because now he is comforting me as I try to read the final chapter openly weeping.

"On behalf of my family, we thank you for taking time out of your lives to come here today to pay your respects to my son. I'm sure you are wondering how I feel. Well I can't explain that to you, but let me tell you a story. When this tragedy happened my first reaction was anger. I was standing in my yard and I just screamed to the top of my lungs – God why did you take my son? A dear friend, a sweet lady, heard this and came to me with a warm embrace and told me that I did not understand. This was God's child. Jarad was only on loan to me for a while."

"This was like giving me the secret formula to an atomic bomb that provided me with the insight into life's master plan. So, I say today that I am extremely honored that of all the men who have ever walked the earth I was chosen to be this young man's father, and for that blessing I will be eternally grateful for the rest of my days. It has been an honor. Most of you know me and some of you know that I have had the good fortune to know great people: CEO's, politicians, international figures, sports stars, entertainers, and all of my heroes. I would always take my son with me during these encounters. He would be there."

"I could feel the sorrow and sadness in the sanctuary as their expressions and tear-filled eyes tugged at my soul. But I continued, "Before we would arrive, I would give him the speech. You know the protocol speech. You have to do this or you had to behave this way or that. He would always look at me in a nonchalant manner and tell me, Dad I got it – don't worry – I got it. When we would get to where we were going, he would fit in perfectly – fit in perfectly. He would fit in perfectly. Now, I said all of that to say this: he will fit in with the angels for all of eternity and of this I am sure."

I found myself quoting Ecclesiastes, which was my grandfather favorite biblical passage: "To everything there is a season and a time to every purpose under the sun. A time to be born and a time to die. …A time to heal; a time to break down, and a time to build up; a time to weep, and a time to laugh; a time to mourn… to love, and a time of peace. Wherefore I perceive that there is nothing better, than that a man should rejoice in his own works; for that is his portion."

This is such a true statement. Particularly, as I looked back on my life and that of the African American experience with my grandson and marvel at the thought that our story is the greatest story ever told. I am personally honored to have given something to everyone whose path I've crossed as I found a place in my heart to care for other souls; especially my very special grandson. I say to him without reservation that I have learned from my suffering and have come to understand the lessons I was taught throughout my life that I now teach you. Just love me as much as I loved you and make sure that you tell your grandchildren about me.

Chapter Nineteen

Sadly the week is over and that special time we've shared is nearing an end, as it is time to take my precious lamb home. I'm so full of joy because of this glorious time we've spent together. As is so often the case, I find myself here at Friendly Church a place where I am so often drawn. The visit with my son is now a ritual for my grandson and I. We slowly walk hand in hand down the slope of the hill in the quiet peaceful cemetery to where his dad rests for eternity. It's important that I bring him here because I am the only connection he has to his Dad.

We slowly make our way to the gravesite. Once there, Boo kneels to pray or as I like to think - talk to his dad. This is always heart wrenching! I have always heard people say that you gain strength from every experience. Particularly, when you have to face life's challenges head on and try to accept the consequence of adversity. I have lived through life's horrors, tried to overcome all that life has put before me, and somehow found a way to endure.

I consider myself blessed or as the good church folk would say, "By the grace of God there go I." Actually, it was by God's grace that I was provided with this vehicle of virtue, which is the only thing that truly raises one man above another. Many people have walked in and out of my life; some with purpose, others with little, and some leaving no impression. Therefore, I am keenly aware and understand that it's up to me to decide who I let stay, who I let walk away, and who I refuse to let go. From this philosophy I've learned that only a true friend will leave a footprint on my heart.

I have come to understand that you can lose money and lose much but when you lose a friend, you lose in the same vain as he who loses faith and that is when you lose all. I can vividly recall my Granddaddy telling me "blessed are those who believe and have not seen. Believe in yourself, follow your heart and live your dreams". Now, Granddaddy never told me it was going to be easy but he did say it will be worth it in the end. In hindsight some of the things he would say at the time seemed so simple. These are the same lessons I teach my grandson as they were taught to me. They will also guide him along the path of his journey as he writes his life's story.

Boo, I want you to learn from the mistakes of others because you will never live long enough to make them all yourself. Remember that beautiful young people are acts of nature but beautiful old people are works of art and that I know to be true. I stress the point, "When you are sad I will dry your tears and when you are scared I will comfort your fears. When you are confused I will help you cope. When you're lost and can't see the light, I will be your shining light of hope. This oath I pledge to you - til the end of my time."

Like my Granddaddy, I too have a favorite biblical passage that I hope my grandson will remember; "Blesseth is the man that walketh not in the counsel of the ungodly, nor standeth in the way of sinners, nor sitteth in the seat of scorners. And he shall be like a tree planted by the rivers of water, that bringeth forth his fruit in his season; his leaf also shall not wither; and whatsoever he doeth shall prosper." This will be the seed I sow, which shall add equity to his tree of life, and my *Legacy and A New Season*".

My grandson has finished talking with his dad and now standing beside me. I take his hand and tell him to remain free in your heart and understand that free is real, free is possible, and free is today. Like any child or should I say out of the month of a babe – he asked, "What is today?" My response was simple coming from the teachings of my grandfather. "Today is the present and a present is a gift. It is a moment in time that is merely an accumulation of many yesterdays that have brought you to now with each minute being the birth place of forever."

The future is a blessing, if it is realized you will understand that we only have a minute, a tiny little minute but an eternity in it. Let me tell you that life's experiences are what define us and it is fear that limits us. It is within the context of that all important minute that we find the wisdom that makes us whole. The wisdom I've shared with you about our past is worthy of great pride but know that history is the past and in spite of the way it is usually told through "His-Story".

At the start of this journey I asked myself a profound question: "If someone, for whatever reason, were to tell the story concealed within my dash. What might they say?" Well, I was blessed to have had *"Just a Season"* to live and fulfill the dreams of those whose broad shoulders I stand upon. I would simply ask that I be judged by the work I've done. I hope that wisdom derived over a span of time transmitted by and received from those who came before me now lives within my grandson.

I felt the need to share this powerful message with my grandson; "Don't stand in someone else's shadow; let your sunlight lead the way." Did Boo understand, probably not, but he listened intently just as I did. It was like history repeating itself. Hence, there is no vestige of a beginning or end as he will pass the baton to continue the Legacy. The most important lesson my Granddaddy thought me was – *education is the single most important ingredient necessary to neutralize those forces that breed poverty and despair.* This philosophy planted the seeds that cultivated a life, which is *"Just a Season."* This too will be the foundation that will create my grandson's book of life.

Our lives are defined based on our memories and those experiences we've endured. The only thing you keep forever is what you give away. As surreal as this moment seemed, an echo of voices surrounded me, causing me to realize that when it's all said and done. I am grateful to have been given the chance to increase the equity within my dash. A warm feeling suddenly engulfs me and to my delight I knew it was the ghosts of Granddaddy, Big Momma, Jarad, and all of those luminous souls who have inspired me say - "Well Done".

I looked at my grandson seeing his sadness, yet I see hope in his eyes. With my arms around him I say, "Do not look at your father's grave and cry for he lives within you. He is not there. He does not sleep. He rests in peace. He was your father and a wonderful son who now belongs to the ages. He is always with you as much as the wind blows. He rest in you like the sunlight on ripened grain. When you wake in the morning's hush he is the swift uplifting rush of a quiet birds circling in flight. Know that he is the soft starlight on a gentle autumn's night that is the reason for your season.

I take his hand and we begin the slow walk up the hill reflecting upon this moment of insight, which is priceless. In the final analysis all that we leave are the precious memories contained within the "Dash" that will be placed between the beginning and end dates of our time. So, it is his mission to increase that equity within your Dash and understand that love is stronger than death.

If you think the battle has been lost remember that defeat is a state of mind. No one is ever defeated until defeat has been accepted as reality. Know that defeat in anything is merely temporary, and its punishment is but an urge for you to reach for a greater effort to achieve your goal. Defeat simply means that something is wrong with what you're doing. Just stay strong in your belief as you continue on the path leading to success.

If you follow the path that God has laid for you, your spirit will live forever, for you are the spring season of my life, and I will live forever through you. If God can be with you, who can be against you, and to that let me just say Amen! We slowly walk past this old familiar place, Friendly Church, as I have done so many times before. I looked at my grandson and said, just as Granddaddy said to me, "fear not for I am with you".

Filled with emotion I look at my grandson and say, if you can keep your head while all of about you are losing theirs – you will inherit the wind and that wind will be my Legacy and A New Season…"

About The Author

JOHN T. WILLS author of the epic novel "Just a Season" has earned a Master's Degree in Business Administration, been a professor, a businessman, past officer of several college, business, and community boards, volunteer and a friend to many. Regardless of the worldly titles given, John prefers to be called a man.

Any accolades the author may have received are attributed to the teachings and solid foundation of a loving grandfather. This man of great wisdom assertively implanted the concept that knowledge is power, which developed into the understanding that education is the single most important ingredient necessary to neutralize those forces that breed poverty and despair.

This philosophy planted the seeds that cultivated a life, which in the final analysis is "*Just a Season*"that has now given rise to "*Legacy – A New Season*".

<u>www.johtwills.com</u>

www.ingramcontent.com/pod-product-compliance
Lightning Source LLC
LaVergne TN
LVHW020631100826
845148LV00012B/2142

* 9 7 8 0 6 1 5 6 5 5 5 0 5 *